EVERY PERSON'S
GUIDE TO
PURIM

EVERY PERSON'S GUIDE TO PURIM

RONALD H. ISAACS

JASON ARONSON INC.
Northvale, New Jersey
Jerusalem

This book was set in 12 pt. ITC Garamond Light by Alabama Book Composition of Deatsville, AL and printed and bound by Book-mart Press, Inc. of North Bergen, NJ.

10 9 8 7 6 5 4 3 2 1

Library of Congress Cataloging-in-Publication Data

Isaacs, Ronald H.
    Every person's guide to Purim / Ronald H. Isaacs.
        p.   cm.
    Includes bibliographical references and index.
    ISBN 0-7657-6046-0 (alk. paper)
    1. Purim. I. Title.
  BM695.P8I73   2000
  296.4'36–dc21   98–21763
                                         CIP

Printed in the United States of America. Jason Aronson Inc. offers books and cassettes. For information and catalog write to Jason Aronson Inc., 230 Livingston Street, Northvale, NJ 07647-1726, or visit our website: http://www.aronson.com

CONTENTS

Contents vii

Contents

Contents

Contents

Contents

Contents

Contents

Contents

Contents

Contents

Contents

Contents

Contents

Contents ix

Contents — ix

PURIM LEGENDS 107

PURIM IN THE SHORT STORY 133
1. Good Purim, Good Purim!! 135
2. Purim Player 139
3. The Sound of the Greggars 142
4. The Purim Rose 146
5. The Purim of Saragosa 150

Notable Purim Quotations 153

Glossary of Purim Terms 159

For Further Reading 163

Index 167

INTRODUCTION

Purim is one of the most joyous of the so-called minor Jewish festivals. The rabbis were so enthralled with Purim that they declared in a maxim, "From the beginning of Adar [the month in which Purim falls] we increase our happiness" (Talmud, *Taanit* 29a).

In its main outline, the story of Purim is typical of the long chain of persecution to which the Jewish people through the centuries have been subjected. Because of a grudge against Mordecai the Jew, the malevolent Haman portrays, to King Ahasuerus, the Jewish people as a dangerous people, scattered and dispersed throughout the empire and refusing to obey the king's laws. A lot (*pur*, in Hebrew) is cast, and the day of the massacre is scheduled for the thirteenth of the month of Adar. After the intervention of Queen Esther, the cousin of Mordecai, a new act is promulgated by the king, giving the Jews the right to organize for self-defense.

The festival of Purim was instituted in commemoration of this event. It derives its name from the Hebrew word *pur* (lot) and is celebrated on the fourteenth day of Adar. The annual celebration of Purim helped the Jewish people, during the dark days of their history, to maintain their trust in the ultimate deliverance from the dangers and difficulties besetting them.

Merrymaking, feasting, and masquerading, characteristic of Purim, have served as a much needed relief from the serious life led during the greater part of the year. At the mention of Haman during the public reading of the Scroll of Esther in the synagogue, it is customary to blot out the name using noisemakers, musical instruments, and even one's feet.

In the course of our history, Jewish communities of different lands have instituted local Purims to commemorate miraculous deliverances from the hands of oppressors. There is the Egyptian Purim on the twenty-eighth of Adar, which the Egyptian Jews observe in commemoration of their deliverance from the hands of the Pasha Ahmed Shitann. The twentieth of Adar commemorates the Frankfort Purim, recording the rescue of the Jews in 1616 by Friederich von der Pfalz. To this day the modern celebration of Purim has made Jews conscious of the spiritual values that their position as a minority group should lead them to evolve and of the perils that they must always be prepared to overcome if they expect to survive as a people. It is perhaps for this reason that the rabbis said that even when all of the other festivals are abolished, Purim will remain (*Midrash*, Proverbs 9:2).

Every Person's Guide to Purim will introduce you to the many facets of the festival of Purim throughout Jewish history. Included will be the history of Purim, its celebration both in the home and synagogue, Purim laws and customs, special Purim commemorations around the world, commentary on the Book of Esther, Purim curiosities, Purim songs, Purim legends, notable Purim quotations, and Purim in the short story. The book will also include a Purim glossary of terms and a listing of books for further reading and research.

The Book of Esther (8:16) states that "for the Jews there was light and gladness, joy and honor." May these same words always describe your Purim festivities and celebration in the years ahead. And remember, too, when it's Adar, be happy!

—Rabbi Ronald Isaacs

Purim in History

ORIGINS OF PURIM

According to many modern Bible scholars, the festival of Purim did not have its source in the story told in the Book of Esther. According to Hayyim Schauss, Purim originally appeared among the Persian Jews and was adopted by them from their non-Jewish neighbors. The Jews of Persia observed, along with their neighbors, an annual festival that was celebrated in the middle of the last of the winter months. From the beginning it had the characteristics of a spring masquerade and was a festival of merriment, play, and pranks. A very popular festival with both Persian and the Babylonian Jewry, it eventually spread to Palestine.

Theodore Gaster presents several theories for the origin of Purim in his volume *Festivals of the Jewish Year*. In one theory, Purim is asserted to date back to the Babylonian New Year Festival. On this day, the gods were believed to determine the fate of men by lot, and the Babylonian word for lot was *puru*. It was also postulated that the festival was characterized by a ritual pantomime that portrayed the conquest of Babylonian gods over those of its neighbors. The problem with this theory is that the Babylonian New Year Festival fell in Nisan (April), not in Adar (March), and it lasted a full ten or eleven days.

Another theory starts from the fact that both the ancient Greek version of the Bible (the Septuagint) and the historian Josephus call the festival not Purim but "Furdaia," which is contended to be a distortion of the Old Persian "Farwadigan," a feast held toward the end of the month of March. The fact is, however, that the Feast of Farwadigan lasted at least five days and was primarily a commemoration of the dead.

A third theory connects the name Purim with the Hebrew word *purah*—"wine press," and assumes that the festival arose in the Greek period as an adaptation of the Greek festival of *Pithoigia*, or "Opening the Wine Casks." Again, this theory has its problems. The opening of wine casks occurs in the fall rather than in the spring, and the plural of the word *purah* is *purot*, not *purim*.

Gaster concludes that the story of Esther is not a historical fact and that the reason for associating it with the feast of Purim could have been that the details of the feast were conveniently explained. He points out that the original form of that feast had these components: the selection of a new queen, corresponding to the selection of Esther; the parade of a commoner qua king, corresponding to the parade of Mordecai in the streets of Shushan (Esther 6:11); a fast, corresponding to Esther's fast (4:15–16); the execution of a felon, corresponding to the hanging of Haman (Esther 7:10, 9:25); and the distribution of gifts (Esther 9:22). Furthermore, that festival must have taken place around the time of the vernal equinox, for it is then that Purim occurs.

All of these aforementioned conditions are satisfied if one assumes that the festival of Purim dates back to an earlier pagan New Year festival. Indeed, at New Year it is customary in many parts of the world to appoint a new ruler in order to symbolize the renewal of communal life. Likewise, the installation of a commoner as temporary ruler between the end of one year and the commencement of another was quite commonplace. The Babylonian New Year was also known to feature a type of scapegoat ritual whereby a condemned criminal was led through the streets in a processional. Finally, there indeed was a custom of distributing gifts at the New Year, as there is today on Purim.

Some scholars have suggested that the Scroll of Esther was written long after the Persian period and was a kind of historical novel intended to comment on the situation of the Jews under Hellenistic rule.

In any event, whatever the true history of the festival of Purim, it had long become established by the second century of the Common Era when a whole tractate of the Talmud, called the *Megillah*, was devoted to the details of the observance.

PURIM IN RABBINIC THOUGHT

There are a plethora of rabbinic opinions related to the festival of Purim and the biblical characters appearing in the Scroll of Esther. Following is a compendium of various opinions as culled from rabbinic literature:

1. **Ahasuerus:** The identity of the Persian King Ahasuerus in the Book of Esther has never been definitely ascertained. The talmudic tractate of *Megillah* 11a identifies Ahasuerus as Xerxes (485–465 B.C.E.). In the *Midrash* (*Esther Rabbah* 1) Ahasuerus is identified as Artaxerxes. There is another rabbinic tradition (*Seder Olam Rabbah* 30) that Cyrus and Darius were the only proper names of Persian royalty. All the other Persian names mentioned in the Bible are merely titles.

Midrash Aba Gorian identifies Darius as the father of Ahasuerus. Accordingly, Ahasuerus was equated with Xerxes I.

Rabbi Levi identified Ahasuerus with Artachshasta (*Esther Rabbah* 1).

2. **Mordecai:** A considerable number of talmudic rabbis seem to have favored the view that it was Mordecai who had been deported in 597 B.C.E. The major reason for this tradition was undoubtedly the fact that a man named Mordecai is listed among those who had accompanied Zerubbabel on his journey to Palestine in 538 B.C.E. (Ezra 2:2). He was commonly identified with the Mordecai of the Book of Esther (Talmud, *Menachot* 65a). The rabbis also interpreted the name Bilshan, listed after Mordecai in the Book of Ezra, not as the proper name of a person but as a noun, meaning "linguist." Thus, the text called him "Mordecai, the linguist." This gave rise to the tradition that Mordecai had been a member of the Sanhedrin prior to his deportation. It was

generally assumed that a linguistic qualification was a prerequisite to an appointment to the Sanhedrin (Talmud, *Megillah* 13b).

Rav Nachman identified Mordecai with the prophet Malachi (Talmud, *Megillah* 15b).

3. **Authorship of the Scroll of Esther:** The authorship of the Book of Esther was attributed by the Talmud (*Bava Batra* 15a) to the Men of the Great Assembly, which was traditionally founded by Ezra and Nehemiah.

4. **Jew:** The Book of Esther (2:5–6) seems to give the name Jew a national connotation by calling Mordecai a Jew because he had come from Jerusalem, where he had been a Judean national. The rabbis suggested that he was called a Jew because he had defended monotheism (*Esther Rabbah* 5).

5. **Hathach:** Rav in the Talmud identified Hathach (Esther 4:5) with Daniel (Talmud, *Megillah* 15a).

6. **Feast of Ahasuerus:** Rabbi Solomon Alkabez (sixteenth century), author of *Lecha Dodi*, asserted in his commentary on the Book of Esther that the feast of Ahasuerus was concluded on the eighth of Nisan. The banquet of Ahasuerus, which was concluded on the eighth of Nisan, had commenced 180 days earlier, on the eighth of Tishri. This sheds some light on the rabbinic statement that Ahasuerus ordered the feast because he had become convinced that Solomon's Temple would never be rebuilt and that the precious vessels of the Temple would remain in his custody (Talmud, *Megillah*

11b). According to Rabbi Nehemiah (*Esther Rabbah* 2:3), the feast began three years after the suspension of the construction of the Second Temple.

7. **Opposition to Purim:** The Babylonian Talmud (*Megillah* 7a) mentions a social objection offered by opponents of the new festival of Purim. There was a fear that the celebration of Purim might provoke gentile resentment. The Jerusalem Talmud (*Megillah* 1) also mentions a religious objection. The objection was based on Deuteronomy 13:1, which prohibits the introduction of new religious laws. The latter objection did not, however, turn out to be a serious bar to the acceptance of Purim in view of the early decision by the Men of the Great Assembly, who had reconciled the establishment of Purim with Mosaic law (Talmud, *Megillah* 7a).

8. **Reading of the *Megillah*:** According to the Talmud (*Megillah* 14a), the prophets instituted the practice of reading the Scroll of Esther. Another talmudic statement (*Megillah* 2a) attributes to the Men of the Great Assembly the designation of the days when the *Megillah* is to be read. The early reading of the *Megillah* was not necessarily a reading of the Scroll of Esther itself but a recitation of events recorded in the Scroll of Esther. It is unlikely that the *Megillah* was recited in the synagogues prior to the canonization of the Book of Esther. The Jerusalem Talmud (*Megillah* 2) implies that the custom of reading the Scroll of Esther in the synagogue was first introduced in the second century of the Common Era, in the time of Judah the Prince, editor of the *Mishnah*. According to the Talmud (*Megillah* 3a), some parts of the

Scroll of Esther were read in public in Jerusalem in the first century of the Common Era.

9. **Canonization of the Book of Esther:** The famous Dead Sea Scrolls, which, according to most historians, date from the first century B.C.E., include fragments from all the biblical books except the Book of Esther. This might well indicate that the Book of Esther had not yet been canonized at that time and consequently had not yet gained a wide circulation. By the fourth century of the Common Era, the practice of the reading of the *Megillah* was so well-established that we are told that the demand for the scrolls was great enough that the scribes supplied them at the low rate of one *zuz* each (Talmud, *Bava Batra* 155b).

10. **The Septuagint and Purim:** The Septuagint is the Greek translation of the Bible. In the very early period after the establishment of Purim, the people relied on oral accounts of the contents of the Book of Esther and also on the Septuagint. The Septuagint referred to Purim as the festival Fruria ("days of protection") and not Purim. It also omits the verse that describes Haman's casting of lots (*hipil pur*), to which the name Purim is attributed in the Book of Esther.

11. **Disputes in the Reading of the Scroll of Esther:** Three *tannaim* of the second century are engaged in a dispute as to which portion of the Scroll of Esther must be read on Purim in order to fulfill the requirements of the Purim ritual (Talmud, *Megillah* 19a). In the Talmud (*Megillah* 6b) we learn of another dispute

in which the second century sages Rabban Simon ben Gamliel and Rabbi Eliezer ben Yosi argue whether the *Megillah* is to be read a second time in the leap month of Adar II if it had already been read in Adar I.

12. **The Scroll of Esther and the Song of the Sea:** The Talmud (*Megillah* 14a) ascribes the reasons for the prophets' decree of the reading of the *Megillah* to a comparison of the Song of Moses recited by the Jews after the crossing of the Sea of Reeds. The Exodus from Egypt and the emancipation from slavery had been commemorated from time immemorial by a special recitation of the Passover story. It was justly felt that the festival of Purim, commemorating the redemption of the Jews from death, should be observed in similar fashion.

13. **The Greek Reading of the *Megillah*:** Widespread use of the Greek Scroll of Esther is reflected in the view of Rabban Simon ben Gamliel, who sanctioned the reading of the Scroll of Esther in the Greek language (Talmud, *Megillah* 18a).

14. **Canonization of the Book of Esther:** The canonization of the Book of Esther was an important turning point in the ritual of the public reading of the *Megillah*. Circumstantial evidence points to the era of Rabban Gamliel II (80–118) as the period when many of the postexilic customs took their final shape. The ritual of the lighting of the Hanukkah *menorah* was fixed, and the Purim miracle was to be publicized through the reading of the Book of Esther. Rabbi Akiva declared that the Book of Esther was written by divine inspiration

(Talmud, *Megillah* 7a). This statement, according to some commentators, led to the canonization of the Book of Esther. It has been asserted that the actual canonization of the Scroll of Esther took place in the second century of the Common Era, in the concluding years of Rabban Gamliel's patriarchate.

15. **Women and the *Megillah*:** In the Talmud (*Megillah* 4a), we learn of the obligation of women to listen to the reading of the *Megillah*.

IN THE SYNAGOGUE

There are a variety of synagogue customs related to the festival of Purim. They actually commence on the Sabbath preceding the festival itself. The special Sabbath preceding Purim is known as Shabbat Zachor: The Sabbath of Remembrance. On this Sabbath, an additional Torah portion is read from Deuteronomy 25:17–19. This Bible reading deals with the injunction to remember (*zachor*) the horrendous attack of Amalek upon the Israelites. Its connection to Purim lies in the fact that according to tradition, Haman was related to the Amalekites, archenemies of Israel.

The special *Haftarah* for the Sabbath of Remembrance is taken from the First Book of Samuel 15:1–34. It deals with Amalek's aggression against Israel during the time of King Saul. The Prophet Samuel tells Saul to retaliate against Amalek for all of the cruelties perpetuated upon the Israelites. As mentioned previously, Haman, who wished to totally annihilate the Jews of Persia, was a descendant of Amalek.

Fast of Esther

The day immediately preceding Purim, the thirteenth of
Adar, is a fast day. If Purim falls on a Sunday, the fast day
is observed on the preceding Thursday. Unlike the fast
of Yom Kippur, the Day of Atonement, which is observed from sunset to sunset, the fast of Esther begins
with daybreak and lasts till sunset, during which time
food and drink of any kind are forbidden, but not such
physical conveniences as bathing. The fast is called the
Fast of Esther and is connected with the fast in the Book
of Esther. When Mordecai informed Esther of Haman's
plans, she asked him to proclaim a three-day fast (Esther
4:16).

It has been suggested that the institution of the Fast of
Esther is of comparatively late origin as it is not mentioned in halachic literature until the eighth century.
According to rabbinic tradition, the fasting of Esther
occurred during the month of Nisan, soon after Haman's
casting of lots. It has further been noted that the Fast of
Esther was instituted as a counterbalance to the merrymaking of Purim.

Noting that the fast proclaimed by Esther was not on
the thirteenth of Adar, some authorities offer a different
explanation. When the children of Israel gathered together on the thirteenth of Adar to defend themselves
against their enemies, they were in a state of war, and
preparations for war always included a public fast.

One modern commentator suggests that the Jews
fasted on the thirteenth of Adar because they were so
occupied with defending themselves that they had no
opportunity to eat.

Reading of the *Megillah*

The primary synagogue observance connected with Purim is the reading of the Book of Esther, called the *Megillah* ("scroll"). It is traditionally read twice: in the evening, after the *Amidah* prayer of the *Maariv* service and before the *Aleynu*. It is also read in the morning after the Torah reading.

The *Megillah* is read from a parchment scroll that is written the same way a Torah is written—by hand, with a goose quill. If there is no such scroll available, the congregation may read the Book of Esther from a printed text, without the accompanying benedictions.

The Book of Esther is chanted according to a special cantillation used only in the reading of the Book of Esther. If no one is present who knows this cantillation, it may be read without the cantillation, as long as it is read correctly. According to the Code of Jewish Law (*Orach Chayim* 690:9), it may be read in the language of the land. In practice, however, the usual custom is to chant the *Megillah* from the scroll in its original Hebrew.

Before the reading, the custom is to unroll the scroll and fold it so that it looks like a letter of dispatch, thus further recalling the story of the great deliverance. The reading is preceded by three benedictions and followed by one. Following are the blessings both before and after the reading of the *Megillah*:

Three Blessings before Reading the *Megillah*

בָּרוּךְ אַתָּה יְיָ, אֱלֹהֵינוּ מֶלֶךְ הָעוֹלָם,
אֲשֶׁר קִדְּשָׁנוּ בְּמִצְוֹתָיו, וְצִוָּנוּ עַל-מִקְרָא
מְגִלָּה: קהל אמן

Baruch ata Adonai elohenu melech ha'olam asher kidshanu bemitzvotav vetzivanu al mikra megillah.

Praised are you, Adonai our God, Ruler of the universe, Who has made us holy by Your commandments and commanded us concerning the reading of the *Megillah.*

בָּרוּךְ אַתָּה יְיָ, אֱלֹהֵינוּ מֶלֶךְ הָעוֹלָם,
שֶׁעָשָׂה נִסִּים לַאֲבוֹתֵינוּ, בַּיָּמִים הָהֵם, בַּזְּמַן
הַזֶּה: קהל אמן

Baruch ata Adonai elohenu melech ha'olam she'asa nisim la'avoteinu bayameem haheym bazman hazeh.

Praised are You, Adonai our God, Ruler of the universe, Who has brought miracles for our ancestors in days of old and at this season.

בָּרוּךְ אַתָּה יְיָ, אֱלֹהֵינוּ מֶלֶךְ הָעוֹלָם,
שֶׁהֶחֱיָנוּ, וְקִיְּמָנוּ, וְהִגִּיעָנוּ לַזְּמַן הַזֶּה: קהל אמן

Baruch ata Adonai elohenu melech ha'olam she-hecheyanu vekeemanu veheegeeyanu lazman hazeh.

Praised are You, Adonai our God, Ruler of the universe, Who has kept us in life and sustained us, enabling us to reach this season.

Blessing after Leading the *Megillah*

בָּרוּךְ אַתָּה יְיָ, אֱלֹהֵינוּ מֶלֶךְ הָעוֹלָם, הָרָב אֶת-
רִיבֵנוּ, וְהַדָּן אֶת-דִּינֵנוּ, וְהַנּוֹקֵם אֶת-נִקְמָתֵנוּ, וְהַמְשַׁלֵּם
גְּמוּל לְכָל-אוֹיְבֵי נַפְשֵׁנוּ, וְהַנִּפְרָע לָנוּ מִצָּרֵינוּ. בָּרוּךְ אַתָּה
יְיָ, הַנִּפְרָע לְעַמּוֹ יִשְׂרָאֵל מִכָּל-צָרֵיהֶם, הָאֵל הַמּוֹשִׁיעַ:

Baruch ata Adonai elohenu melech ha'olam harav et reevaynu vehadan et deenaynu vehanokeym et neek-matenu vehameshalaym gemul lechol oyayv nafshaynu vehaneefra lanu meetzareynu. Barch ata Adonai haneefra le'amo yisrael meekol tzarayhem ha'el ha-mosheeya.

Praised are You, Adonai our God, Ruler of the universe, Who does contend for us, judge our cause, and avenge our wrong, Who renders retribution to our mortal enemies, and on our behalf deals out punishment to our adversaries. Blessed are You, O God, Who on behalf of Your people deals out punishment to all their adversaries, O God, the Savior.

Customs during Reading of the *Megillah*

The *Megillah* must be read standing and from the scroll, not by heart. During the reading, there are four special verses, called "verses of redemption" (*pesukei ge'ulah*), which are said aloud by the congregation and then repeated by the reader. Here are the verses of redemption:

i. Now in Shushan, the palace, there was a certain Jew, whose name was Mordecai, the son of Yair, the son of Shimei, the son of Kish, a Benjamite (Esther 2:5).

ii. And Mordecai went out from the presence of the king in royal apparel of blue and white, and with a great crown of gold, and with a garment of fine linen and purple. The city of Shushan rejoiced and was glad (Esther 8:15).

iii. The Jews had light, and gladness, and joy, and honor (Esther 8:16).

iv. For Mordecai the Jew was next to King Ahasuerus, and great among the Jews, and accepted of the multitude of his brethren, seeking the wealth of his people, and speaking peace to all his seed (Esther 10:3).

At certain key points in the Book of Esther it is a custom for the reader to raise his or her voice, adding drama to the story. Here are these key verses:

i. For he sent letters into all the king's provinces, into every province according to the writing thereof, and to every people after their language, that every man should bear rule in his own house, and that it should be published according to the language of every people (Esther 1:22).

ii. And let the maiden which pleases the king be queen instead of Vashti. And the thing pleased the king, and he did so (Esther 2:4).

iii. And the king loved Esther above all the women, and she obtained grace and favor in his sight more than all the virgins; so that he set the royal crown upon her head, and made her queen instead of Vashti (Esther 2:17).

iv. For if you altogether hold your peace at this time, then shall there be enlargement and deliverance arise to the Jews from another place. But you and your father's house shall be destroyed. And all who knows whether you have come to the kingdom for such a time as this? (Esther 4:14).

v. And Esther answered: If it seems good to the king, let the king and Haman come this day to the banquet that I have prepared for him (Esther 5:4).

vi. On that night the king could not sleep, and he commanded to bring the book of records of the chronicles. And they were read before the king (Esther 6:1). [Note: This verse is considered to be the turning point of the entire story in the Book of Esther.]

Another interesting part of the chanting of the Book of Esther is the four verses (Esther 9:7–10) enumerating the ten sons of Haman. The custom, already mentioned in the Talmud (*Megillah* 16b), is for the reader to chant the names of Haman's sons in one single breath, in order to signify that they died together. Other reasons for this custom included the fact that we should avoid the appearance of gloating over their fate, even though it was deserved.

It is a widespread custom for the listeners at the *Megillah* reading to make noise, usually with special noisemakers called greggars, or in Hebrew, *ra'ashanim*, whenever Haman's name is mentioned. Some congregations also encourage the use of wind and percussion instruments as noisemakers. The custom of blotting out the name of Haman appears to be the outgrowth of a custom once prevalent in France and Provence, where the children wrote the name of Haman on smooth stones, then struck them together whenever Haman was mentioned in the reading so as to rub it off, as suggested by the verse "the name of the wicked shall rot" (Proverbs 10:7).

Many modern-day congregations today are known to hold concurrent readings of the *Megillah*, each reading specially tailored to a particular age group or level of understanding. The singing of Purim songs during the reading of the *Megillah*, dressing up in costume, and other acts of frivolity are also part of today's modern *Megillah*-reading festivities.

Synagogue Purim Services

The services on Purim are the same as on the other weekdays except for a few variations. The "*al hanissim* paragraph" is added in both the *Amidah* prayer and in the Grace after the Meals. The following is a translation of this prayer:

> We thank You for the heroism, for the triumphs, and for the miraculous deliverance of our ancestors, in other days and in our time. In the days of Mordecai and Esther, in Shushan, the capital of Persia, the wicked Haman rose up against all Jews and plotted their destruction. In a single day, the thirteenth of Adar, the twelfth month of the year, Haman planned to annihilate all Jews, young and old, and to permit the plunder of their property. You, in great mercy, thwarted his designs, frustrated his plot, and visited upon him the evil he planned to bring on others. Haman, together with his sons, suffered death on the gallows he had made for Mordecai.

During the morning services on Purim, the Torah is read. The reading is from Exodus 17:8–16, describing Joshua's victory over the people of Amalek with the sword. Amalek, you will recall, was said to have been related to Haman, and thus the choice of this reading for Purim morning.

Interestingly, unlike Hanukkah, the *Hallel* psalms of praise are not recited on Purim. The rabbis sought to understand the reason why. The Talmud explains that the redemption represented by Purim was not complete. True, the Jews were saved from the annihilation plotted by Haman, but they still remained subject to Ahasuerus (Talmud, *Megillah* 14a), whereas after the redemption commemorated by Passover, they ceased to be subjects of Pharaoh, and after Hanukkah they were no longer subject to Antiochus. Others explain that the reading of the *Megillah* performs the function of *Hallel*, while the Talmud also explains that *Hallel* is not said for events that took place outside the Land of Israel.

The day after Purim (i.e., the fifteenth of Adar) is known as Shushan Purim, referred to in the Book of Esther (9:18) as the day when the Jews of Shushan, capital of Persia, celebrated their triumph. It is celebrated as a semi-holiday. The *Tachunun* prayers of supplication are not to be recited at synagogue on this day.

Purim in a Leap Year

During a leap year, it is the usual practice to do all things that must be done during the month of Adar during the First Adar, in conformity with the talmudic principle that "one must not pass by precepts" (Talmud, *Pesachim* 64b). Purim, however, is celebrated only during the Second Adar.

PURIM IN THE HOME

The following verse from the Book of Esther provides the basis for all the practices ordained and adopted in connection with Purim, with the exception of the reading of the *Megillah*:

> And Mordecai wrote these things, and sent letters to all the Jews that were in all the provinces of the king Ahasuerus both near and far, to enjoin them that they should keep the fourteenth day of the month of Adar, and the fifteenth day of the same, the days wherein the Jews had rest from their enemies, and the month which was turned unto them from sorrow to gladness and from mourning unto a good day; that they should make them days of feasting and gladness, and of sending portions to one another and gifts to the poor. (Esther 9:20–22)

The "feasting and gladness" are expressed by the special Purim *seudah* meal, an especially festive meal held in the afternoon before sundown. In order to heighten the joy at this meal, the rabbis even allowed an unusual amount of levity. Well-known is the statement in the Talmud: "Rav said: A person should be so exhilarated with drink on Purim that he does not know the difference between 'cursed be Haman' and 'blessed be Mordecai'" (Talmud, *Megillah* 7b). The later rabbinic authorities tried hard to lessen the exuberance of this command. Because they could not condone intoxication, they suggested that the passage really means that one may drink more than one does usually. It was also ingeniously suggested that the numerical value of "cursed be Haman" (*arur Haman*) and "blessed be Mordecai" (*baruch Mordecai*) are the same. To be unable to discover this does not require a very high degree of intoxication. Naturally, it was necessary to know when the one was called for and when the other. Again, one did not have to be highly intoxicated to confuse the responses.

The permissiveness in regard to drinking on Purim was explained on the grounds that drinking was very much involved in the story of Purim. Vashti herself fell from grace when "the heart of the king was merry with wine" (Esther 1:10), which resulted in Esther becoming the queen. When Esther became queen, there was a similar banquet (Esther 2:18), and Haman's own downfall started with the drinking of wine.

It was customary in Eastern Europe for young children at the Purim *seudah* to be disguised in costumes and sing humorous Purim songs or render humorous dramatic recitations, usually of their own composition. Each country and each generation, dating back to talmudic times, had its own form of merrymaking.

In many European countries, where a carnival of parades, pantomimes, and masquerades took place at about the same season of the year, the celebration of Purim was influenced by the customs of the environment. Consequently, on this day plays were produced representing scenes from the events related in the *Megillah* and, at times, also from other biblical stories.

The amateur players were known as Purim *shpielers*, with women often dressed in the garb of men, and vice versa. This type of dress would normally have been forbidden, but it was permitted in the case of Purim because the object was merrymaking.

In America, not counting the reading of the *Megillah*, the celebration of Purim found its widest expression in synagogue religious schools. It is in the schools that we have Purim plays, carnivals, masquerade contests, and Queen Esther crownings. Some adult organizations also sponsor Purim masquerade balls and parties.

In the State of Israel, Purim has experienced a great revival, with emphasis on the national theme. One specific innovation is the *adla-yada*. The name is based on the talmudic statement in which one is allowed to drink so as to be so exhilarated with drink that one does not know (*ad dela yada*) the difference between "cursed be Haman" and "blessed be Mordecai." It is an elaborate, well-organized parade with floats, bands, marchers, costumes, and dancing in the streets and squares of the city. Such floats are also seen today in Borough Park, Brooklyn, New York, a community known for its traditional Jewish families and many Hasidic sects.

Mishloach Manot: Purim Gift Giving

Another Purim practice is that of *mishloach manot* (Code of Jewish Law, *Orach Chayim* 695:4). Here, the custom is for families to exchange gifts of food and pastries. The custom of giving gifts to the poor on Purim has become a casualty of our modern system of organized charities. In ages past, it was ordained that on Purim people were to be extra-generous, giving to all who asked without question. It is still customary in some synagogues to put collection plates on a table in the vestibule of the synagogue. The contributions are called *machzeet hashekel* money, in commemoration of the half-shekel that was collected in ancient days around the time of Purim for the upkeep of the Temple in Jerusalem.

Hamantachen

The only special food for Purim is *hamantachen*, a three-cornered pastry traditionally filled with poppy seeds (the original name was *muntashen—mun* being the Yiddish word for "poppy seeds"). In Hebrew, this pastry is called *oznay haman*, based on the older name *Haman Ohren*, or in Italian, *Orrechi d'Aman*. In old illustrations Haman is often pictured wearing a three-cornered hat, and this may have given rise to the three-cornered pastry.

Family Activities

Purim Seudah

The most popular traditional family activity on the afternoon of Purim is the Purim *seudah* meal. It is a time for family and friends to gather, usually late in the afternoon on Purim day rather than at lunchtime. In some communities families that sponsor a Purim *seudah* ask that all participants come dressed in costume. Purim skits often take place at the meal, as does a custom called "Purim *torah*." Purim *torah* consists of various forms of mocking the tradition by designing a variety of parodies. Quiz questions with humorous answers are also a popular Purim *seudah* pastime as well as the singing of Purim songs that often parody a variety of subjects. Here are a few sample parodies and activities that you may wish to use at your Purim *seudah*.

A. **Purim Bible Quiz**

1. What time of day was Adam created? Answer: A little before Eve.

2. Who in the Bible slept five in a bed? Answer: David. He slept with his forefathers.

3. Where is there proof in the Bible that Joseph played tennis? Answer: Joseph served in the courts of Pharaoh.

4. Where is baseball mentioned in the Bible? Answer: In the big inning (beginning).

5. Where is baseball mentioned in the Book of Psalms? Answer: "Who can understand his errors?" (Psalms 19).

6. Why was Haman hung on a tree? Answer: He was guilty of treezon.

B. **Purim Talmud**

Mishnah: One should get so drunk on Purim that one does not know the difference between "blessed be Mordecai" and "cursed be Haman."

Gemarah: Rabbi Mendel commented: Does this mean that people should not get drunk together, for the *Mishnah* clearly states that *"one* should get drunk"? May I suppose that more than one may not get drunk? Rabbi Samuel retorted: What do you think? What is the fun of getting drunk by yourself? Is it not taught in the Holy Bible, "One who gets drunk by himself is like one who studies the unholy books."

Rabbi Pilpul added: The *Mishnah* clearly states that only *men* need get drunk, for it says "so that *he* does not know the difference." Rabbi Judy answered him in kind: "What is the fun of man's getting drunk if a woman does not also get drunk?" Rabbi Pilpul was silenced.

Rabbi Tuvia commented: Why does the *Mishnah* state "blessed be Mordecai" before "cursed be Haman?" Could it not have been stated in the opposite order? And is it not the truth that *acharon acharon chaviv* ("the last is dearest")? Rabbi Joseph responded: The author of the *Mishnah* would have put the verses in the opposite order had he remembered the saying "last is dearest." However, since he was already drunk when he composed the *Mishnah*, he forgot the verse "last, etc."

C. **Purim Humor**

The following joke is typical of Purim humor:

The patriarch Abraham wanted to upgrade his PC to Windows 95. His son Isaac was incredulous.

"Pop, you can't run Windows 95 on your old, slow 386! Everybody knows that you need a Pentium or at least a fast 486 with a minimum of 16 megs of memory in order to multi-task effectively with Windows 95."

Abraham, the man of faith, gazed calmly at his son and replied: "God will provide the RAM, my son."

D. **Purim Play** (written by Barbara Cohen)

Here is a play that you may wish to use or adapt for use at your Purim *seudah* or at your synagogue during the reading of the *Megillah*.

Chapter 1

Ahasuerus: In the third year of my reign, I, Ahasuerus, King of the Medes, and the Persians, made a great feast for all my princes, and for all the people who lived in Shushan, my capital.

Vashti: And at the same time, I, Vashti, the Queen, made a feast for all the women in the royal house.

Ahasuerus: I drank a lot of wine. To tell the truth, I was drunk. I ordered my servants to bring Vashti before my guests, so they would see how beautiful she was.

Vashti: But I didn't want to be exhibited before the crowd like a freak in a sideshow. So I sent the servants back with a message for the King. "I will not come!"

Ahasuerus: What shall we do with the Queen? How shall she be punished for refusing to obey me?

Memucan: Her disobedience is a shame and a disgrace. It will set a bad example for all the women of Persia. You must send her away. Take another wife. Make her your new Queen.

Ahasuerus: So be it.

Chapter 2

Mordecai: I, Mordecai, a Jew, lived in Shushan with my cousin Esther. She was an orphan, and I took care of her as if she were my own daughter. She was beautiful and fair to look upon.

Memucan: O mighty King, bring all the beautiful young girls of your kingdom here to Shushan. Look them over, and then pick the one you like the best for your Queen.

Ahasuerus: So be it.

When the king's decree was published, Esther had to go to the king's house, like all the other maidens.

Mordecai: Esther, don't tell anyone that you're a Jew. I'll walk near the king's house of women, to find out how you're getting on.

Esther: When it was my turn to go before the king, the king's servants offered me ointments, cosmetics, jewelry, and fine clothes. But I required none of these.

Ahasuerus: Oh, Esther, you are lovelier in both body and soul than any of the other women. I make you my Queen, and with my own hands I set the royal crown of Persia upon your head.

Mordecai: I sat in the king's gate, and I overheard Bigtan and Teresh plot to kill the king. I told what I had heard to Esther, and Esther told the king. Bigtan and Teresh were hanged on a tree and all that had happened was written by the scribe in the king's book.

Chapter 3

Haman: Then was I, Haman, appointed to be the king's chief advisor. I required that all the people bow down to me, as if I were the king himself. You there, you, Mordecai. How come you aren't bowing?

Mordecai: I am a Jew. I bow down to no man.

Haman: I'll get Mordecai for this. I'll get not only Mordecai, but his people, the Jews. I have cast *purim*, lots. The lot fell in the month of Adar. Then will I have revenge on all the Jews.

Ahasuerus: What is it that you want, Haman, chief of all my princes?

Haman: There is certain people scattered throughout your kingdom. They have their own laws. They could be dangerous. If you will allow them to be destroyed, I'll pay ten thousand pieces of silver into the king's treasury.

Ahasuerus: Here is my ring. Do as you will.

Haman: I, Haman, in the name of the king, proclaim this: On the thirteenth day of the twelfth month, which is the month of Adar, destroy all the Jews, both young and old, men and women and little children.

Chapter 4

Mordecai: Esther, do you know what Haman has done? He has issued a decree over the king's seal. All the Jews of Persia are to be killed. Esther, you must go before the king. You must beg him to save our people.

Esther: Don't you know the law of this kingdom? Any man or woman who has not been sent for and yet appears before the king is put to death—unless the king holds out his golden scepter. I haven't been called to come to the king for a whole month.

Mordecai: Don't think you'll escape if all the other Jews are killed. Who knows? Perhaps you were made queen for just such a time as this.

Esther: Gather together all the Jews of Shushan. Tell them to fast for me. I and my maidens will also fast. And then I will go to the king. If I die, I die.

Chapter 5

Esther: My lord the King, I kneel before you.

Ahasuerus: And I extend my golden scepter to you. What do you want, Queen Esther? Whatever you request, even if it's half my kingdom, I will give it to you.

Esther: My lord, this is my request. If I have found favor in your sight, let the king and Haman come to a banquet that I shall prepare for them tomorrow night.

Haman: How wonderful! How marvelous! I'm rich. I have ten sons. I'm promoted higher than any other man in the kingdom. And now the queen invites only me to come with the king to a banquet she has prepared herself. But all this means nothing to me so long as I see Mordecai the Jew sitting in the king's gate.

Zeresh: Let a gallows be made of fifty cubits high, and tomorrow speak to the king that Mordecai be hanged on them. Go with the king to the banquet.

Haman: What an excellent idea. I will ask the king's permission this very night.

Chapter 6

Ahasuerus: I can't sleep. Scribe, read to me from the Book of Records and Chronicles.

Scribe: Mordecai told of the two doorkeepers who sought to kill the King.

Ahasuerus: How was Mordecai rewarded for his good deed?

Scribe: There is nothing done for him.

Ahasuerus: Who is in the court?

Scribe: Haman stands in the court.

Ahasuerus: Let him come in. Haman, what shall be done to a man the king wishes to honor?

Haman: It must be me. Let the man be dressed in the king's clothes. Let him mount the king's horse. And let the most noble prince in the land lead him through the streets crying, "Thus is it done to the man whom the king wishes to honor!"

Ahasuerus: Hurry now and do just that for Mordecai!

Haman: Oh, my wife, I did it. I did just that for Mordecai. I had no choice.

Zeresh: If Mordecai is a Jew, as you have said, you won't triumph against him. Oh, no. Surely you will fall before him.

Chapter 7

Esther: Welcome, O mighty king. Welcome Haman. Welcome to my banquet.

Ahasuerus: What is it that you want, Queen Esther? It will be granted to you, even if it's half my kingdom.

Esther: If you love me, O king, let my life be given to me, and the life of my people, for we are sold, I and my people, to be destroyed, to be slain, to perish.

Ahasuerus: Who is he, and where is he, that dares to threaten you?

Esther: He is here, this enemy, this wicked Haman. He brought the Jews, to kill them. My lord, I am a Jew.

Haman: O my queen, I throw myself at your mercy. I beg you to spare me.

Ahasuerus: What? Do you dare to attack the queen before my very eyes?

Scribe: Look in the court. There is the gallows fifty cubits high that Haman made for Mordecai.

Ahasuerus: Hang Haman on that gallows.

Chapter 8

Ahasuerus: To you, Esther, my Queen, I give all of Haman's property and wealth. And to you, Mordecai, Esther's cousin, I give the ring I took back from Haman.

Esther: Mordecai, I set you over the house of Haman. My king, if it pleases you, and if you love me, and if it seems right to you, reverse the letters sent out by Haman ordering the Jews to be destroyed. How can I bear to see the destruction of my people?

Ahasuerus: Writings in the king's name and sealed with the king's seal cannot be reversed. But send out whatever additional letters you wish, and seal them with my seal.

Mordecai: Then let it be told to all the Jews that they are to fight for their lives, and destroy any who would attack them.

Ahasuerus: You, Mordecai, shall go among the Jews of Shushan wearing the royal tunic of blue and white, and a great crown of gold upon your head, and a robe of fine linen and purple.

Esther: And all the Jews of Shushan will be glad.

Chapters 9 and 10

Mordecai: On the thirteenth day of the month of Adar, the Jews gathered themselves together, and they slew all their enemies who would have destroyed them, and the ten sons of Haman were hanged upon the gallows.

Esther: And on the fourteenth day of the month of Adar the Jews rested and made it a day of feasting and gladness.

Mordecai: I sent letters to all the Jews in all the provinces of King Ahasuerus, both near and far, to keep the fourteenth day of the month of Adar every year as a day that was turned from sorrow to gladness, a day that was turned from mourning into a good day. I told them to make it a day of feasting and gladness and of sending portions to one another, and to the poor.

Esther: Then Mordecai and I wrote down all that had happened in a book so that the days of Purim would be kept every year by our children and our children's children, and our children's children's children.

Ahasuerus: I, King Ahasuerus, advanced Mordecai so that he became second in the kingdom only to me. All of his deeds are written down in the chronicles of the Kings of Media and Persia. For Mordecai sought the good of his people and peace for all those who came after him.

Baking Hamantachen

Baking *hamantachen* as a family can be a fun-filled activity. Here is a recipe for you to try:

1 pound vegetable shortening
5 cups flour
1 teaspoon salt
1 cup pineapple juice
$\frac{1}{2}$ cup sugar

Mix and refrigerate roll of sugared flour. Cut and fill. Bake at 400 degrees for 20–25 minutes.

Cream Cheese Filling

$\frac{3}{4}$ cup brown sugar
3 ounces cream cheese
$\frac{1}{2}$ teaspoon salt
1 teaspoon vanilla
$\frac{1}{2}$ cup either nuts, chocolate chips, coconut, or brickle

Best if chilled. Mix all ingredients. Fill dough and bake.

Playing Purim Games

Here is one game to get you started on your way. (You will find several other games in the chapter on Purim games in this volume.) Called the Packing Shushan game, its purpose is to have family members share their knowledge of Purim with one another. These are the instructions:

a. One person begins by saying, "I pack my trunk with a Purim costume." The next player, "I pack my trunk with a Purim costume and a greggar." The third person must repeat the first two objects and add an additional one, such as, "I pack my trunk with a Purim costume and a greggar and a mask." Each person repeats all of the items previously mentioned in order and adds a new one.

b. A player who fails to correctly repeat the list is eliminated from the game. The game continues until the contents of the trunk are too numerous to remember.

The Book of Esther

The Scroll of Esther, known as the *Megillah*, is chanted in the synagogue on the eve of Purim and again the next morning. It is the last of the five scrolls that form part of the third division of the Bible, known as the *Ketuvim*, or Writings. *Megillat* Esther tells the story of the salvation of the Jews of the Persian Empire. The Scroll of Esther is universally known as the *Megillah*, not because it is the most important of the five scrolls, but due to its immense popularity, the prominence that is given to its public reading, and the fact that it is the only one that is still generally read from a parchment scroll. At one time it was normative for every Jewish household to possess a *Megillah*, and much time and skill were devoted to the production of beautifully illuminated texts and elaborate wooden and silver cases that would house the scroll.

The Story of Esther is a work of much literary merit. The characters are distinctly portrayed and the descriptions graphic, with a remarkable amount of action in its plot.

The Book of Esther has been so very popular among Jews that a vast body of legendary amplification and commentary has grown up around it. There are the apocryphal additions to the book. The ancient historian Josephus, in his *Antiquities*, gives a largely elaborated account of the story. The talmudic tractate of *Megillah* also devotes many pages to a haggadic interpretation of the narrative.

CONTENTS OF THE BOOK OF ESTHER

The Persian King Ahasuerus climaxes one hundred and eighty days of banqueting for his officials with an additional feast of seven days for all of the people of Shushan. On the seventh day of this grand banquet, the king, while clearly intoxicated, orders Queen Vashti to appear so that all may appreciate her beauty. When Vashti refuses, the king removes her from her position, and a contest is subsequently held to choose a successor to Vashti. One of the women taken to the palace is Esther (a.k.a. Hadassah), the cousin of Mordecai, the Jew. Esther, concealing her origins, finds favor with the king and is chosen as the new queen of Ahasuerus.

Mordecai soon learns of a plot against the king devised by two of his eunuchs. He reveals this to Esther, who in turn informs the king. The eunuchs are executed in the second chapter of the book.

Ahasuerus now elevates Haman the Agaggite, a descendant of Agag (king of the Amalekites), and all of the king's courtiers bow down to Haman in recognition of his high rank. Mordecai refuses, on the grounds that he is Jewish. Angered by this snub, Haman resolves to exterminate Mordecai and the entire Jewish people and determines the appropriate day by lot (*pur*). He then convinces the king that the Jews are a treasonous people who should be eliminated. King Ahasuerus then authorizes Haman to deal with the Jews as he sees fit. Haman writes to all of the royal governors, appointing the thirteenth of Adar for the mass extermination of the Persian Jews (Chapter 3).

Learning of this decree, Mordecai appeals to his cousin Esther to intercede with the king. In spite of the potential danger to her of appearing before the king without being specifically invited, Esther agrees to spend three days fasting and then to go to the king (Chapter 4).

On the third day, Esther approaches the king and is spared. She now requests that the king and Haman come to a banquet that night. At the banquet, Esther refuses to reveal her true wishes, but merely asks that Ahasuerus and Haman attend a second banquet that she will give the following night. Haman returns home, proud of being so honored. At the advice of his wife and supporter, he prepares a gigantic stake upon which to hang Mordecai (Chapter 5).

Because the king cannot sleep that night, he orders that the royal annals be read, and thereby discovers by chance that Mordecai had never been properly rewarded for denouncing the two eunuchs who had previously plotted against the king. He asks Haman's advice concerning a means of honoring someone whom the king deems worthy of honor. Haman, incorrectly thinking that he himself is the chosen one, proposes a procession in royal garb upon a royal horse and proclaiming: "This is what is done for the man whom the king desires to honor." The king then orders Haman to do this for Mordecai (Chapter 6).

At the second banquet, Esther denounces Haman for plotting the destruction of her people. When Haman appeals to Esther for mercy, the king, thinking he intends to ravish her, orders him to be hanged on the same stake prepared for Mordecai (Chapter 7).

Haman's place in the king's favor is now taken over by Mordecai, but Haman's decree sealing the fate of the Jews poses a dangerous problem, because, according to the Persian constitution, a royal decree may not be revoked. Mordecai, however, writes to all of the governors and other important officials authorizing the Jews to defend themselves and to destroy anyone who may attack them (Chapter 8).

Mordecai's prestige is apparently sufficient to insure that the royal officials favor the Jews on the fateful day. Instead of a Jewish extermination, the Jews kill five hundred of their enemy as well as the ten sons of Haman in Shushan, and seventy-five-thousand enemies in the provinces. At the request of Esther, the Jews are given the fourteenth of Adar to avenge themselves of their enemies.

The days following the battles (the fourteenth and fifteenth of Adar) are declared by Mordecai and Esther to be days of feasting and merrymaking, and they are designed as "the days of Purim" in memory of the lots (*purim*) that Haman cast (Chapters 9 and 10).

AUTHORSHIP AND HISTORICITY
OF THE BOOK OF ESTHER

The Book of Esther claims to be a simple historical account of events that actually took place in Shushan. It is true that there was a Persian king named Ahasuerus, for Ahasuerus is merely a Hebrew form of the Persian name that the Greeks heard as Xerxes. It is also true that an ancient tablet was found that speaks of a royal official named Marduka, or Mordecai, at about the same time of the rule of Xerxes I. Finally, the author of Esther seems quite well-acquainted with Persian customs and court practices, as is illustrated by Vashti's refusal to degrade herself and appear at the drinking party. A Persian wife left when the drinking began!

Nevertheless, to accept the Book of Esther as the historical truth involves many chronological and historical difficulties. If, for example, Mordecai was exiled from Judea with Jehoiachin (589 B.C.E.) as Esther 2:6 suggests, he would have been over one hundred years old at the time of the reign of Xerxes I. In addition, the plot is filled with many improbabilities, including the wondrous ability of Queen Esther to conceal her nationality and religion.

The Talmud (*Bava Batra* 15a) ascribes the authorship of the Book of Esther to the men of the Great Assembly. Rashi, the medieval commentator, ascribes the authorship to none other than Mordecai himself.

A significant group of scholars consider Esther, much like Daniel, a pseudepigraph, in which the narrative set in Persia is merely a stage setting for the true meaning. One scholar (Willrich) suggests that Ahasuerus is really

Ptolemy Euergetes II (170–164 B.C.E.) and Esther, his queen, is Cleopatra III, who was friendly to the Jews.

Another school of thought bases its interpretations on the fact that the names of Mordecai and Esther are derived from the names of the Babylonian deities Marduk and Ishtar. This approach sees the story as an account of the conflicts of these gods or of their worshipers.

Indeed, any analysis of the Book of Esther makes it difficult to propose a specific date for its author. Nevertheless, quite a number of modern-day Bible scholars have established a few facts upon which all agree. The author of the Book of Esther was a Persian Jew, possibly from Shushan. He wrote before 78 B.C.E., the date the Greek translation of the Book of Esther was brought to Egypt, and before the composition of the Second Book of Maccabees 15:36, which mentions the fourteenth of Adar as "the Day of Mordecai."

CANONIZATION AND THE GREEK VERSION OF THE BOOK OF ESTHER

One direct result of the non-Jewish atmosphere that pervades the Book of Esther was the refusal of some of the rabbis to admit Esther into the Jewish canon. The Talmud (*Megillah* 7a) preserves debate on whether Esther was written with the proper divine inspiration and whether it defiles the hands, like other biblical works. Indeed, the major objection to including Esther in the canon seems to have been the lack of clear references to God. Ultimately, of course, the book was admitted, and it now comprises one of the thirty-nine books of the Jewish Bible, called the *Tanach*.

The Book of Esther was translated into Greek by Lysimachus, son of Ptolemy of Jerusalem. His translation was brought to Egypt in the fourth year of the reign of Ptolemy and Cleopatra.

Interestingly, the Greek translation contains six passages not found in the Hebrew text. These passages add a religious element, specifically prayer, to the book to help explain theologically how and why the Jews were saved. A particular interpretation of the conflict between Haman and the Jews is also emphasized. Haman's decree, according to the Greek version, charges the Jews with exclusiveness and disloyalty, which endangered the state. The Jews, in Mordecai's decree, answer that their God is the ruler of the world Who takes and gives away kingdoms.

MUSICAL RENDITIONS
OF THE BOOK OF ESTHER

The traditional view that the Book of Esther should be read like a letter has greatly influenced its musical rendition. There is also the traditional practice of changing the motives or the tempo when especially gladdening or sad events come to be narrated. The melody motif used for the Book of Esther is very near to that used for the Book of Ruth, with the addition of motives from the Song of Songs and the borrowing of motives from the Book of Lamentations.

Purim in Jewish Law and Custom

The following are a few laws and customs related to the festival of Purim and the reading of the *Megillah*, as culled from the Code of Jewish Law (Condensed Version).

THE READING OF THE *MEGILLAH*

1. As soon as the month of Adar arrives, our joys increase. If a Jewish person has a lawsuit with a non-Jew, he should go to court during this month.

2. In the days of Mordecai and Esther, the Jews gathered on the thirteenth of Adar to defend themselves against, and seek retribution of, their enemies. They had to ask for mercy from the Holy Blessed One, that God might help them. And we find that when the Jews were at war, they fasted, so that God might help them. Also, our teacher Moses fasted when he waged war against the

49

Amalekites. It is therefore presumed that also in the days of Mordecai and Esther they fasted on the thirteenth of Adar. Therefore, all the Israelites have taken upon themselves to fast on the thirteenth of Adar. This is known as the "Fast of Esther." This fast is to remind us that the Holy Blessed One hears the prayers of every man in time of distress when he fasts and returns to God with all his heart, as God heard the prayers of our forefathers in those days. However, this fast is not as imperative as the four fasting days that are mentioned in the Scriptures. Hence, we may be lenient about this fast on occasion.

3. Purim is the fourteenth of Adar. If Purim occurs on a Sunday, the fast is advanced to Thursday. If a circumcision takes place on Thursday, the feast should be held at night, but the *sandek* and the father of the infant are permitted to eat in the daytime, and they are not required to make up for the fast on Friday. But if any other person forgets and eats on Thursday, he must fast on Friday.

4. To show reverence for the *Megillah*, we should put on our Sabbath clothes in the evening, and on returning home from the synagogue, we should find the lights lit, the table set, and the beds made. In the evening after the *Amidah*, the whole *Kaddish* is said, including *titkabel*. Then the *Megillah* is read.

5. Before Purim begins, it is customary to donate half the unit coin current in the country, to commemorate the half-shekel the Jews used to give in the month of Adar

for buying of the public sacrifices. The general practice is for every person to give three half-shekels, because in the Torah portion of *Ki Tissa* (Exodus 30:11–16), the word *termuah* ("offering") is mentioned three times. It is given in the evening before the *Megillah* is read, and the money is distributed to the poor. A minor is exempt from contributing the half-shekel, but if his father has once contributed for him, he must continue to do so. Some authorities hold that a lad of thirteen must donate it, while others hold that he is exempt up to the age of twenty.

6. In the *Shemoneh Esreh* of the evening, morning, and afternoon service, we include *al hanissim* ("for the miracles").

7. Everyone, man and woman, is obliged to hear the *Megillah* both in the evening and in the morning. Hence, maidens, too, should go to the synagogue. Those unable to go to the synagogue should hear the reading of the *Megillah* at home. Children, too, should be trained to hear the *Megillah*. Nevertheless, very young children should not be taken to the synagogue lest they disrupt the service.

8. At night it is forbidden to read the *Megillah* before the stars appear, even if one is in great distress on account of the fast. But one may have some light refreshments before the *Megillah* is read, such as coffee, and the like, in order to somewhat alleviate the weakening effect of the fast.

9. The precept is best observed if one hears the *Megillah* in the synagogue where there is a multitude of people, for "in the multitude of people is the king's glory" (Proverbs 14:28). One should at least try to hear it read in a *minyan* of ten. But if it is impossible to obtain a quorum of ten, each individual should read it out of a valid *Megillah* and say the benedictions that precede it. If one of them knows how to read it and the others not, that one should read it and the rest should listen, and their obligation is thus fulfilled.

10. It is an established custom that the reader spreads out the *Megillah* and folds it, folio upon folio, like a letter, because the *Megillah* is designated as *iggeret* (a letter of Purim) (Esther 9:29). The listeners are not required to spread their *Megillot*.

11. The reader of the *Megillah* should intend to exempt all the listeners from reading it, and the listeners should fulfill their obligation. Therefore, they must listen to every word, for should they fail to hear even one word, their obligation would not be fulfilled. The reader is thus required to cease reading while there is noise and confusion at the mention of Haman and to wait until the commotion is entirely over. Nevertheless, it is fitting and proper for each worshiper to own a valid *Megillah*, so that he himself may say, word for word quietly, as perchance he might fail to hear one word from the reader.

12. The reader should recite the names of the ten sons of Haman, including the word *aseret* (ten) all in one

breath, to indicate that they were all hanged at one time . . . In the evening, when the reader says (Esther 6:1): "In that night the king could not sleep," he should raise his voice, for at that verse the story of the miracle begins. When the reader says (Esther 9:29), *iggeret happurim* ("the letter of Purim"), he should wave the *Megillah*.

13. One who has a *Megillah* that is not valid, or a Bible, should not recite the words together with the reader, because he should not listen well to the reader, and even if he himself could pay attention, someone else might listen to him and not to the reader. Nor should anyone vocally assist the reader; therefore, the reader must repeat the four terms of redemption, "light, gladness, joy, and honor" (Esther 8:16), which the congregation reads aloud.

14. If one who has already fulfilled the obligation of reading the *Megillah* is reading it for the benefit of others, then the listener himself should say the benedictions if he is able to do so. If it is read for the sake of a woman, it is best that the leader should say the following benediction: "Who has sanctified us by His commandments and has commanded us concerning the *listening* of the *Megillah*."

15. In a city that has been surrounded by a wall since the days of Joshua, the son of Nun, the *Megillah* is read on the fifteenth of the month of Adar.

THE SENDING OF PORTIONS—
GIFTS TO THE NEEDY—PURIM *SEUDAH* (FEAST)

1. On Purim it is the duty of everybody to send no less than two gifts to one of his friends, for it is written (Esther 9:22): "And of sending portions to one another," which means two gifts to one. The more gifts one sends to his friends, the more praiseworthy one is. Nevertheless, it is better to give charity to the needy than to make a great feast and to send gifts to one's friends. There is no greater joy and no more glorious deed before the Holy Blessed One than the gladdening of the hearts of those in need, the orphans and the widows. And one who gladdens the hearts of those unfortunates is likened to the Divine Presence, of whom it is written (Isaiah 57:15): "To revive the spirit of the humble, and to revive the heart of the contrite."

2. "Portions" to friends must be gifts of food that can be eaten without further preparations, such as boiled meat, fish, confectionery, fruits, wine, or something similar.

3. Everybody, even the poorest person in Israel who is himself dependent on charity, is to give at least one gift each to two poor persons, for it is written (Esther 9:22): "And gifts to the poor," which means, two gifts to two poor persons. One should not make any inquiries in giving to the poor. Whoever puts out his hand and begs should be given alms. If one lives in a community where there are no poor people, one must either keep the

Purim money until one meets poor persons, or send it to some needy persons that he knows.

4. Women, too, must send gifts to their friends and contribute to charity on this day. Women should send gifts to women, and men to men, but as regards charity to the needy, women may help men, and men may help women. Some women depend on their husbands that they give for them as well. But this is improper; they should be more exacting about it.

5. Purim must be celebrated by eating, drinking and making merry. Also, on the night of the fourteenth of Adar, one must be joyful and eat somewhat more abundantly. If Purim occurs on Saturday night, although one must have a third meal on the Sabbath, one should eat a little less during the day in order to be able to enjoy the Purim repast. Nevertheless, the obligation of feasting on Purim is not fulfilled by the feast that we make at night. The principal Purim feast is to be held in the daytime. For it is written (Esther 9:22): "Days of feasting." It is appropriate to light candles as becomes a festival occasion, even though the meal occurs in the daytime. On the night of the fifteenth, there should also be some rejoicing. The giving of charity and the sending of gifts to friends should be performed during the daytime. And because people are concerned with sending out portions, a part of the repast is taken in the nighttime.

When Purim occurs on Friday, the feast is held in the morning, in deference to the Sabbath. It is well to engage in the study of Torah for a short time before beginning the feast. A support for this view is found in the verse

(Esther 8:16): "The Jews had light," and "light" is defined as having reference to the Torah. Some authorities say that it is appropriate to eat some seeds on Purim, to recall the seeds that Daniel and his comrades ate in Babylon, and also to recall the seeds that Esther had eaten. For the Talmud (*Megillah* 16b) says: "The verse [Esther 2:9]: 'And he advanced her and the maidens to the best,' means that he permitted her to have seeds for her food."

6. The whole miracle of Purim was occasioned through wine: Vashti met her fate at the wine feast and Esther took the crown in her stead. The downfall of Haman was due to wine. Therefore, the Sages, of blessed memory, made it obligatory on every one to become drunk, and ordained: "One is obliged to regale himself on Purim, until one is unable to differentiate between 'cursed be Haman' and 'blessed be Mordecai.'" At least to commemorate the great miracle, one should drink more than one is accustomed, until one falls asleep, and while asleep, one will be unable to differentiate between "cursed be Haman" and "blessed be Mordecai." However, if a person has a delicate constitution, likewise if he knows that drunkenness may cause him, God forbid, to slight some precept, a benediction, or a prayer, or that it will lead him, God forbid, to levity, it is best for him not to become intoxicated. For all our deeds must be for the sake of Heaven.

7. A mourner, even during the first seven days of mourning, is obliged to send gifts to the needy and portions to his friends. He should not, however, send them anything that will cause joy. But we do not send any-

thing to a mourner the entire twelve months, even a thing that is not of a joy-provoking nature.

8. No labor may be performed on Purim, and whoever performs any labor on that day will never derive any benefit from it. But it is permissible to have work done for us by a non-Jew. It is also permissible to attend to business, to write even a social letter, to make a note of debts due, and to do anything that does not require much concentration. It is especially permissible to write something of a religious nature or do some work for the performance of a precept. For the requirements of Purim it is permissible to perform any labor.

9. The fifteenth of Adar is known as Shushan Purim. On this day it is forbidden to deliver funeral orations or to fast. It is customary to make festive meals and to be merry on Shushan Purim. Marriages are permitted on this day, but not on the fourteenth of Adar, when the *Megillah* is read, for it is a joyous event, and we do not join one festive event with another.

The following are some laws of Purim as cited in Maimonides' Code of Law, the *Mishneh Torah*, Laws of Purim.

1. We are bidden by the sages to read the *Megillah* at its proper time. It is widely known that this reading was prescribed by the prophets. Everyone is required to hear its reading: men, women, proselytes, and emancipated slaves. Minors should be trained to read it.

2. The sages prescribed several dates for the reading of the *Megillah* because it is written "at their appointed times" (Esther 9:31). These are the dates for the *Megillah* reading: Every town in *Eretz Yisrael* or abroad that was surrounded by a wall since the time of Joshua, the son of Nun, should read it on the fifteenth of Adar, even if it has no wall at the present. Such a town is referred to as a walled city. Every town that was not surrounded by a wall in the days of Joshua, even if it has a wall now, should read the *Megillah* on the fourteenth of Adar. Such a town is referred to as an open city.

3. Although the castle-city of Shushan was not surrounded by a wall in the days of Joshua, the son of Nun, the *Megillah* is read there on the fifteenth of Adar, because it was there that the miracle occurred, as it is written: "They rested on the fifteenth" (Esther 9:18). This was made to depend on the days of Joshua in deference to *Eretz Yisrael*, which was in ruins at that time. The inhabitants of *Eretz Yisrael* were to be considered residents of walled cities so as to read the *Megillah* at the same time as the residents of Shushan. Although *Eretz Yisrael* is still desolate, its residents are to read the *Megillah* on the fifteenth of Adar in localities that used to be surrounded by defense walls during the period of Joshua. *Eretz Yisrael* is thus remembered in connection with the miracle of Purim.

4. The *Megillah* must not be read on the Sabbath. This is a precautionary measure, lest someone might take the *Megillah* to a skilled reader, transporting it four cubits or more through a public domain.

5. If a man read the *Megillah* by heart, he has not fulfilled his duty. If a speaker of a foreign tongue heard the *Megillah* read from a copy written in the Hebrew language and in Hebrew script, he has fulfilled his duty, even though he did not know what they said. Similarly, if the *Megillah* is written in Greek, and he heard it read, he has discharged his duty, even though he knows no Greek, and even if the listener is familiar with Hebrew.

6. If a person reads the *Megillah* without due intention, his duty has not been discharged.

7. One is required to distribute charity to the poor on Purim. The applicants for Purim money should not be scrutinized. It should be given to anyone who holds out his hand. Purim money must not be diverted to any other charity.

8. One should rather spend more money on gifts to the poor than on his Purim banquet and presents to his friends. No joy is greater and more glorious than the joy of gladdening the hearts of the poor, the orphans, the widows, and the strangers. He who gladdens the heart of these unhappy people imitates God, as it is written: "I am . . . to revive the spirit of the humble, and to put heart into the crushed" (Isaiah 57:15).

9. All Prophetic Books and Sacred Writings will cease to be recited publicly during the messianic era, except for the Book of Esther. It will continue to exist just as the Five Books of the Torah and the laws of the Oral Torah that will never cease. Although ancient troubles will be

remembered no longer, as it is written, "The troubles of the past are forgotten and hidden from my eyes" (Isaiah 65:16), the days of Purim will not be abolished, as it is written: "These days of Purim shall never be repealed among the Jews, and the memory of them shall never cease from their descendants" (Esther 9:28).

PURIM QUESTIONS
AND ANSWERS

Over the years, as a congregational rabbi, I have been asked many questions related to all of the holidays of the Jewish calendar. Following are a cross section of some of the more interesting questions that I have been asked concerning Purim, and the answers that I gave to these questions.

1. Why do we make noise when Haman's name is read from the Scroll of Esther?

Answer: The custom of making noise has a fascinating biblical origin. The Book of Exodus (Chapter 17) describes an intense battle in the wilderness between the Israelites and the soldiers of Amalek. Although Israel prevailed, the Book of Exodus (17:14) records God saying to Moses: "Write this for a memorial in the book . . . I will utterly blot out the resemblance of Amalek from under the heavens." Here God is telling the

Israelites that the descendants of Amalek will always be their enemies and thus to "blot them out."

History has proven to be true, for centuries later Agag, king of the Amalekites, became a bitter enemy of the Jewish people. Agag was eventually executed by the prophet Samuel, and the name of Amalek was blotted out.

The Book of Esther (3:1) identifies Haman as "the son of Hammedatha, the Agaggite"—in short, a direct descendant of Amalek. It is asserted that the author of the Book of Esther deliberately forged a bond between Amalek and Haman so as to accentuate Haman's malevolent character. Remembering the ancient biblical injunction "to blot out" Amalek's name, the Jewish people proceeded to do this on Purim by using noise-makers to blot out Haman's name.

2. What is the history of the *greggar*?

Answer: The word *greggar* is derived from a Polish word meaning "rattle." In about the thirteenth century, European Jews sounded the *greggar* whenever the *Megillah* mentioned the name of Haman.

Centuries before, in talmudic times, Jews would burn Haman in effigy.

3. What is the origin of the Purim *spiel*?

Answer: A Purim *spiel* is a play, originating in about the fifteenth century in Germany. Interestingly, some of these original plays, in the form of spoofs to add to the merriment of the holiday, have been preserved to this day.

4. What is the origin of the Purim costume?

Answer: The festival of Purim borrowed from the pagan carnivals of ancient times, especially from the later Roman carnivals. Beginning in about the fifteenth century, European Jews adapted the costumes and processions of these carnivals for Purim. Children would march through their towns dressed as characters in the *Megillah* story.

Many congregations today sponsor a Purim carnival where children, and adults, too, dress up in costume. Some communities also sponsor masquerade parties.

5. Are you really supposed to get drunk on Purim?

Answer: According to the Talmud (*Megillah* 7b), one should drink until one can no longer tell the difference between "cursed be Haman" and "blessed be Mordecai." This is the only instance of an injunction to get drunk in the whole of Jewish literature, and a variety of commentators argue that it was not, in fact, to be taken literally. But some pious Jews, in their anxiety to obey rabbinic teaching, did take it literally. Maimonides, the medieval commentator, proposed that one should drink enough to become mellow or sleepy. In this state of oblivion, one would be unconscious of the difference between blessing Mordecai and cursing Haman. Some rabbis today monitor the permissiveness to drink carefully, but only as long as individuals do not become abusive or destructive.

6. What is the exact meaning of Purim?

Answer: The Hebrew word *purim* derives from the old Persian world *pur*, meaning "lots." It refers to the "lottery tickets" used by Haman in order for him to determine the date for the destruction of the Jews.

7. Is the story of Esther historically true?

Answer: Probably not, although there is a supposed ancient tomb of Esther and Mordecai in Iran. Historical records of Persia in the fifth century before the Common Era (when the story of Purim appears to take place) makes no mention of Haman, Esther, or Mordecai, nor do they refer to any of the incidents in the Book of Esther. Although many theories of the origins of Purim abound, no one theory is universally accepted, and the real origin of the festival continues to remain a mystery.

8. What is the connotation of the name Esther?

Answer: In Hebrew, Esther connotes "concealing," from the verb *sater*. Queen Esther concealed her identity, nationality, and faith from Ahasuerus and his court until the time was ripe for Haman's exposure.

9. In leap years, why is the observance of Purim deferred to the month of Adar II?

Answer: According to the commentator the Maharil, Purim is to be observed in the Second Adar in a leap year in order to have the celebration of Jewish deliverance from the hands of Haman fall as close as possible to Passover, the seasonal commemoration of freedom from Egyptian bondage.

10. Why are the *Hallel* psalms, chanted on most holidays, not chanted on Purim?

Answer: The reading of the *Megillah* itself is a form of praise for the miracle of Purim. Furthermore, it appears that *Hallel* is never chanted on occasions commemorating a miracle that took place outside the Land of Israel.

11. There is a custom to have circumcision ceremonies held on Purim morning prior to the reading of the *Megillah*. Why is this so?

Answer: The reading of the *Megillah* contains the verse "the Jews had light, gladness and joy . . ." (Esther 8:16). Accordingly, we want the infant initiated into the ranks of the Jewish people by the time this verse is read so that he, too, may be eligible to have a portion in that joy.

12. If Esther fasted for three days, according to the Book of Esther, why is the fast of Esther observed for only one day?

Answer: According to the rabbis, the reason is that a three-day fast would be considered an undue hardship.

13. When Purim falls on Sunday, why is it that the Fast of Esther, usually held the day before Purim, is observed the previous Thursday?

Answer: Two reasons are generally given in rabbinic commentary for the Fast of Esther to be held on Thursday when Purim falls on Sunday. One is that even the preparation for the Sabbath on Friday is characterized by joy. Thus, fasting would impede the joyous Sabbath preparation. Additionally, if people were to fast and spend additional time in prayer and study, they would have little time and strength left for the preparation of the Sabbath.

14. There are five *Megillot* (Scrolls) in the Bible: Song of Songs, Ruth, Lamentations, Ecclesiastes, and Esther. Yet when people speak of the *Megillah*, they are always talking about the Book of Esther. Why?

Answer: The fact is that in the narrative itself the event of Purim is referred to both as *sefer* ("scroll"), as in *sefer Torah* (Esther 9:32), and *iggeret* ("letter") (Esther 9:21). This is why a kosher *Megillah* must be written on parchment and in the same script as a Torah scroll, but when it is read it must be folded like a letter to fit both descriptions.

Purim Oddities and Curiosities

All Jewish holidays have a variety of unusual facts, customs, traditions, and curiosities related to them. Following are some of the more interesting curiosities and oddities related to the festival of Purim.

1. Queen Esther and Hadassah—The Women's Organization: Esther's Hebrew name in the *Megillah* is Hadassah, the same as that of the famous Zionist organization for women. People have often asked whether there is a connection between the organization and Queen Esther's alternate name, Hadassah.

After a visit to Palestine, the great Jewish leader Henrietta Szold decided to form a Zionist organization for women. She envisioned this group working for the health of women and children in what was later to become the modern State of Israel. The founding meeting was held at Congregational Emanu-El of New York. The date was Purim in 1912. The women constituted themselves as the Hadassah chapter of the Daughters of

Zion. Eventually, the name would become simply Ha-dassah.

2. **No God in the Scroll of Esther:** Interestingly, the word for God, although alluded to in a number of places, is not mentioned even one single time. There are many assertions as to why this is so. For instance, the rabbis of the Talmud say that Esther pleaded with the spiritual leaders of her day to record the historical event in which she had been involved, so that future generations might value her supreme dedication to God and her people. The rabbis therefore told the story as a historical event in which Esther was the heroine, and they were not explicit about the part God played in this miracle. So the name of God does not appear in the narrative.

In another explanation we are told that Esther married a non-Jew (Ahasuerus) in the Purim story, and this was God's unique way of saving His people from annihilation. However, people who come to read the Book of Esther could conclude that intermarriage was perfectly acceptable because of this precedent. If God's name were to be included in the *Megillah*, such readers might not realize that God's hand had guided these unique events but would assume that God sanctions intermarriage. Thus, according to this explanation, God was not mentioned in the *Megillah*.

3. **"So They Hanged Haman" (Esther 7:10):** In Yemenite congregations the community usually joins the reader in reciting the verse "so they hanged Haman." The reason for this is that the five-fold expression of redemption used with reference to the Exodus from Egypt was

compared to the terms used in the redeeming of the Jews from the plots of Haman.

4. **Longest Biblical Verse:** The longest verse in the Bible is found in the Scroll of Esther. It is the verse in Chapter 8, Verse 9. The original text contains forty-three Hebrew words. Here is the verse in the translation: So the king's scribes were summoned at that time, on the twenty-third day of the third month, that is, in the month of Sivan; and letters were written, at Mordecai's dictation, to the Jews and to the *satraps*, the governors, and the officials of the one hundred and twenty-seven provinces from India to Ethiopia: to every province in its own script and to every people in its own language, and to the Jews in their own script and language.

5. **Never on the Sabbath:** The day on which Purim is celebrated (fourteenth of Adar) can never occur on the Sabbath. The fifteenth of Adar does occasionally fall on the Sabbath. Thus, the Jews of Jerusalem, who celebrate the fifteenth of Adar, must celebrate a "three-day Purim." On the fourteenth the *Megillah* is read, on the fifteenth the blessing "Who wrought miracles" is recited, and on the sixteenth the Purim *seudah* takes place.

6. **Second Purim:** In a speech of Hitler on January 30, 1944, he said that if the Nazis went down in defeat, the Jews could celebrate "a second Purim."

7. **Persian Purim:** The Jews of Persia celebrate Purim with great splendor because that is where the story unfolded. Religious school children make a life-sized figure

of Haman to be hanged in effigy on Purim. During the reading of the *Megillah*, the children do not use *greggars* when Haman's name is mentioned. Rather, they shoot off fireworks.

8. **Special Purims:** A custom arose that whenever a Jewish community was saved from its enemies, it would celebrate the event annually with a special local Purim. These days were known as Purim Katan—the Little Purim. The celebration was modeled after that of Purim, with fasting the day before, reading a *Megillah* that recounted the story of salvation, reciting the *Al hanissim* prayers, and holding a special feast. The Encyclopedia Judaica lists over one hundred special Purims. Here is a sample of special Purim celebrations:

  i. Purim of Algiers (Purim Edom): Established in 1540 and observed on the fourth of Cheshvan, it commemorates being saved from destruction in the Spanish-Algerian wars of 1516–1517 and 1542.

  ii. Baghdad Purim: Established in 1733 and observed on the eleventh of Av, it commemorates being relieved from Persian oppression in 1733.

  iii. Belgrade Purim: Established in 1822 and observed on the nineteenth of Sivan, it commemorates being saved from destruction during the Turko-Serbian war.

  iv. Cairo Purim (Purim Mitzrayim): Established in 1524 and observed on the twenty-eighth of Adar, it commemorates being saved from extermination.

v. Castille Purim (Purim Martinez): Established in 1339 and observed on the first of Adar, it commemorates being saved from annihilation following accusations by Jew-baiter Gonzales Martinez, the king's advisor.

vi. The Prague Purim: Established in 1620 and observed on the fourteenth of Cheshvan, it commemorates being saved from riots by protection of Emperor Ferdinand II.

vii. Roman Purim: Established in 1793 and observed on the first of Shevat, it commemorates the ghetto being saved from assault and fire.

viii. Sarajevo Purim: Established in 1819 and commemorated on the fourth of Cheshvan, it commemorates the ten leaders of the Jewish community who were freed from prison and saved from execution.

ix. Vilna Purim: Established in 1794 and observed on the fifteenth of Av, it commemorates being saved from destruction during the Russo-Polish war.

x. Galicia Purim: The exact date of its establishment is not known. Observed on the twelfth of Tevet, it commemorates being saved from annihilation because of blood libel accusations.

9. **Family Purims:** Families were also known to establish their own family Purim commemorations that were related to having been saved from some terrible decree. For instance, the Altschul family of Prague estab-

lished its family Purim in 1623 (observed on the twenty-second of Tevet). On this date, the head of the family, Chanoch Moses, was saved from death. The family of Samuel HaNagid of Spain established its special family Purim in 1039, observing it on the first of Elul. On this date the family was saved from the death plot of conspirators.

10. **Day of Nicanor:** The day before Purim is on the thirteenth of Adar. The thirteenth of Adar is also mentioned in the Talmud as the day on which vengeance was executed (during the time of the Hasmoneans) against a tyrant who oppressed the land of Judah. The name of the tyrant was Nicanor, who fell by the hand of Judah, the son of Mattathias, on the thirteenth of Adar.

11. **Queen Esther Street:** There is a Queen Esther Street in Tel Aviv. There are also Esther towns in the state of Missouri and in the state of Louisiana.

12. **Mordecai's Day:** According to the Second Book of Maccabees 15:36, Purim was known as Mordecai's day.

13. **Let's Party:** In the Book of Esther, the Hebrew word *mishteh* ("party" or "banquet") occurs some twenty times.

14. **One of a Kind:** The Book of Esther contains several words that appear only once in the whole Bible. Here are several of them:

Tevet, the tenth Hebrew month (Esther 2:16)
Kasher, meaning "fit" or "proper" (Esther 8:5)
Karpas, a Persian word meaning "cotton" (Esther 1:6)

15. **The Whole Alphabet:** All of the letters of the Hebrew alphabet can be found in Chapter 3 of the Book of Esther, Verse 13.

16. **Samaritan Purim:** The Samaritans hold their Purim festival in the month of Shevat, to commemorate Moses' mission to help to free the Israelites from Egypt.

17. ***Adloyada* Carnival:** In Tel Aviv beginning in the 1920s, the custom grew of having, on Purim afternoon, a parade and carnival called *Adloyada* from *ad lo yada*—"until you do not know." This is derived from the talmudic injunction to drink until you don't know the difference between "cursed be Haman" and "blessed be Mordecai." Part of the festivities in Tel Aviv is to choose a Queen Esther as part of a real beauty pageant.

18. **Mohntaschen:** The three-cornered pastries (*hamantachen*) were originally called in Yiddish *mohntaschen*—"poppy seed pockets." This is because the pastries were filled with poppy seeds (*mohn*, in Yiddish).

19. **Chickpeas and Queen Esther:** One of the traditional dishes at the Purim *seudah* is chickpeas. Queen Esther herself is said to have eaten them in the king's palace in order to avoid eating nonkosher foods.

20. **Purim Folk Blessing:** Traditional Eastern European Purim tables are adorned with a gigantic Purim

challah, or *koiletch*. It is so big that it has given rise to this folk blessing. After someone had sneezed four or five times in a row and *gesundheit* was clearly unavailing, the Eastern European Jews would say: *Tzu voksen tzu kvellen vi lahng und vi breit vi a Purim loiletch*—"May you feel good and grow big, as long and as broad as a Purim challah."

21. **Messianic Purim:** According to rabbinic tradition, all the festivals will one day no longer exist, but the days of Purim will never cease, continuing into the Messianic Age.

22. **Yom Kippurim and Purim:** The Day of Yom Kippur contains the word Purim. Many commentators have seen similarities between the two. For instance, on both days we step outside ourselves completely, one to rise, one to fall. Then we step back in and get back to the business of life.

23. **Hidden Hand of God:** Concealed in the Book of Esther, rabbinic commentators have discovered many signs of God's Presence. For example, in the Book of Esther, the name of God (YHVH) is formed by the initial letters of four successive words when read backward: *Hee vechol hanashim yitnu*—"it, and all the women will give." In the Book of Esther, the name of God (YHVH) is formed by the final letters of four successive words when read backward: *Zeh aynenu shoveh li*—"this gives no satisfaction to me."

Finally, the word *yehudeem*, Hebrew for "Jews," occurs thirty-eight times in the Book of Esther. Thirty-two times it is spelled in the traditional way: *yod-he-vav-dalet-yod-mem*. The other six times, however, an extra letter *yod* is inserted before the final letter *mem*, so that there are two *yod*s together (Esther 4:7, 8:1, 8:7, 8:13, 9:15, and 9:18). Some commentators assert that the extra *yod* in six places is intentional, alluding to God's Presence. First of all, the letter *yod* itself means *yad*, "hand." And two *yod*s in succession are a common abbreviation for "God." Together, it is posited, the combined meaning of the double *yod* is "the hand of God."

24. **Purim Legendland:** There are many legends connected with Purim. Following are some statements of Purim in Legendland:

a. Haman hated the Jews because a Jewess (Esther) had taken the place of Vashti, who was his sister.

b. Haman hated Mordecai because he at one time had been Mordecai's barber and slave.

c. The name Esther was another name for Venus.

d. Mordecai had kept Esther hidden for four years before he had allowed her to go to the king's palace.

e. All the trees of the forest had refused to give their wood for Haman's gallows on which to hang Mordecai, until only the thornbush agreed and offered its wood.

f. During the night when the chronicles were read to him, two angels threw the king out of his bed 365 times in order to keep him awake.

PURIM SONGS

Singing and merrymaking are very much a part of the Purim celebration. Following are some of the festive songs, both traditional and recent, that are sung both in the synagogue and at the Purim *seudah* during the festival.

1. ***Shoshanat Yaakov***: The famous Purim song *Shoshanat Yaakov* alludes to the biblical verse: "The city of Shushan shouted and rejoiced" (Esther 8:15). The name *Shoshanat Yaakov*, therefore, refers to the descendants of Jacob who lived in Shushan. By extension, medieval Hebrew poets referred to the Jewish people in general as a *shoshana* ("rose").

> *Shoshanat ya'akov tzahalah v'samechah,*
> *Birotam yachad techelet mordecai*
> *Teshu'atam hayita lanetzach*
> *Vetikvatam bechol dor vador.*
> *L'hodiah shekol kovecha lo yevoshu*

Velo yikalmu kol hachosim bach.
Arur haman asher bikesh l'abdi
Baruch mordecai yehudi
Arurah zeresh eshet mafchidi
Berucha ester ba'adi
Vegam charvonah zachur latov.

The Jews of Shushan beamed with joy
When they beheld Mordecai robed in blue.
You have always been our deliverance
Our hope in every generation.
Those who set their hope in You will never be put to
     shame.
Those who trust in You will never be confounded.
Cursed be Haman who sought to destroy us.
Blessed be Mordecai, the Jew.
Cursed be Zeresh, the wife of the one who terrified us;
Blessed be Esther, our protector,
And may Charvonah also be remembered for good.

2. *Chag Purim*

Chag Purim chag Purim
Chag Gadol hu layhudim
Masechot veraashanim
Zemirot rikudim
Hava narisha
Rash rash rash
Baarashanim.

The holiday of Purim
Is a great one for Jews
Masks, noisemakers, song, and dance.
Let's make noise with our *greggars.*

3. *Ani Purim*

Ani Purim ani Purim
Sameiach umvadeach
Halo rak pa'am bashana
Avo lehitareach
La la. . . .

Heidad Purim heidad Purim
Haku tof umtziltayim
Hoi mi yiten uva Purim
Lechodesh lechodshayim
La la la. . . .

I am Purim, I am Purim
Happy and making jokes
Only one time in the year
I will come to be your guest
La la. . . .

Hurray Purim, hurray Purim,
Beat the drum and tambourine
I wish that Purim would continue
For one month or two.

4. *Zemer LaPurim*

Chavraya hayom Purim
Yom chag simcha lakol
Hava nagil nismach
Venaytzay bemachol
Nishkach laregel kat
Saval u'de'agot
Ma'agal gadol na'aseh

Nirkod belee hafugot.
Ronu tzahalu
Shiru ad beli dai
Ve'nareh lakol
Ki amenu chai.

Today is Purim brothers,
A happy holiday.
Rejoice and be merry,
Dance in a ring.
Turn the *greggars*, dance and sing.

5. *Zeh Hayom*

Zeh hayom Purim
Ma naim umatov
Zemirot nezamay venishmach ad en sof
Smach mordecai smach
Hatzarot na shechach
Lanetzach lo nishkach hanes
Hoi shiru nashir
Ki bushushan haman ha'agagi az met

This is Purim, fellows,
A joyous holiday,
With songs and cheers and hellos.
Let's wend our merry way.
Laugh, comrades, laugh
Eat hearty and quaff,
Marvel at God's wondrous way
Sing, comrades, your song.
Dance merry in throngs
Remember that wonderful day.

6. *Utzu Eitza*

Utzu eitza vetufar
Dabru davar velo yakum
Ki imanu el.

You may scheme and plot against us
But to no avail.
For God is with us.

7. *Shu shu shu shu shu shushan* (to the tune of "Polly Wolly Doodle All Day")

Oh, Haman was a high and mighty bluff
In Shu-shu-shu shu-shushan long ago.
He ordered Mordecai to take his derby off
In shu-shu-shu-shu-Shushan long ago.

But Mordecai sat and laughed in his face
In shu-shu-shu-shu-shushan long ago.
So Haman swore he'd exterminate his race
In Shu-shu-shu-shu-Shushan long ago.

Chorus

Oh Esther was a timid little maid
In Shu-shu-shu-shu-Shushan long ago.
But Mordecai told her she needn't be afraid
In Shu-shu-shu-shu-Shushan long ago.

Chorus

So she went to the King and she gave him a smile
In shu-shu-shu-shu-Shushan long ago.

The King, he liked her manner and her style
In Shu-shu-shu-shu-Shushan long ago.

Chorus:

Ahasuerus was a jolly little king
In Shu-shu-shu-shu-Shushan long ago.
He ordered Haman to take a long swing
In Shu-shu-shu-shu-Shushan long ago.

Chorus:

So we sing, so we sing
So we sing and raise a row
For Haman he was swinging
While Mordecai was singing
In Shu-shu-shu-shu-Shushan long ago.

8. **A Wicked, Wicked Man**

Oh, once there was a wicked, wicked man
And Haman was his name, sir.
He would have murdered all the Jews
Though they were not to blame, sir.

Chorus:

Oh, today we'll merry merry be (3)
And *nash* some *hamantachen*.

And Esther was the lovely queen
Of King Ahasuerus.
When Haman said he'd kill us all
Oh, my how he did scare us.

Chorus:

But Mordecai, her cousin bold,
Said, "What a dreadful 'chutzpa.'"
If guns were but invented now
This Haman I would shoot, sir."

Chorus:

When Esther speaking to the King
Of Haman's plot made mention.
"Ha ha," said he, "Oh, no, he won't!
I'll spoil his bad intention."

Chorus:

The guest of honor he shall be
This clever Mr. Smarty
And high above us he shall swing
At a little hanging party.

Chorus:

Of all his cruel and unkind ways
This little joke did cure him.
And don't forget we owe him thanks
For this joyous feast of Purim.

Chorus:

9. **It's Purim, It's Purim** (to the tune of "A Tisket, a Tasket")

It's Purim, it's Purim
A happy day is Purim.

Haman got it in the neck
And that is why we're happy.
Queen Esther, Queen Esther,
A pretty maiden was Esther.
She wrecked the plot that Haman planned
And that is why we're happy.
Hamantachen do we eat,
At Haman's mention stamp our feet,
Shalach manot do we send,
To tyranny there comes an end.
It's Purim, it's Purim
A happy day is Purim.
The villain died
He must have fried
And that is why we're happy.

10. **Hey, Jews** (to the tune of "Hey, Jude")

Hey, Jews, when times are bad,
Don't you worry, things will get better
Remember to keep the faith in your heart
Then you can start to make it better.

Hey, Jews, don't be afraid
You were chosen to be God's people.
Remember that bigotry is a sin,
Then you begin to make it better.

And any time you feel the pain, hey, Jews, refrain,
From hiding your faith, assimilating.
For now you know, you should be proud, proclaim out
    loud
You're willing to fight to stop the hating.

Haman was feeling down
He said, "I know what is the matter.
I'll ask to murder all of the Jews,
The king won't refuse, then I'll feel better."

So Haman told it to the king, who liked the thing
And placed its enforcement on his shoulders.
But when Ahasuerus knew who was a Jew
He realized his bedroom could get colder.

Hey Jews . . .

11. **He's a Real Ha-a-man**

He's a real Haman
Sitting high in Shushan land
Making all his evil plans
For you and me.

He's as blind as he can be,
Just sees what he wants to see,
Haman, do you know the queen at all?

Haman, please listen:
You don't know what you're dissin'.
Haman, the empire is at your command.

Doesn't have the slightest clue
Who he'll have to answer to
When he tries to push the Jews into the sea.

Haman should worry
He could lose in a hurry
At the ball, when Esther the Queen spoils his plans.

12. **Estherday** (to the tune of "Yesterday")

Estherday, all my troubles
Seemed so far away,
Then that wicked Haman had his say.
Oh, how we longed for yesterday.

Suddenly, we were victims of his bigotry.
Due for slaughter on Adar 14
Our fate has changed quite suddenly.

Then, Queen Ester came
With her uncle Mordecai.
They said: "This can't be,
We will have to stop that guy."

Purim day, we remember they spoke up to say
Discrimination must be swept away
On Mordecai and Esther day.

PURIM GAMES

PURIM CHARADES

The central part of the evening Purim service is the reading of the *Megillah*. A game that can be played at the Purim *seudah* and involve the entire family is Purim Charades. Charades combines many elements, which make it an almost universal favorite.

First of all, it is a guessing game. There is a mystery to be solved, one every few minutes. Everyone enjoys a mystery and especially delights in being the quick-witted or lucky one to solve it first. Charades is also an acting game. We are all born actors, and we all enjoy make-believe. This universal play impulse is completely satisfied in acting out the charades. Here is a description of the Purim Charades Game.

Purpose: To reenact famous expressions and events related to the Purim holiday

Group: Ages 10 and up

Time: 30–45 minutes

Materials

   1. Purim expressions related to the Scroll of Esther and festival customs

   2. A watch with a second hand is also useful for timing the charade.

Instructions

   1. Divide the players into two teams. Give the first player on team one the first charade. Tell him that he will have two minutes to present nonverbal clues in order to get his team to correctly identify the expression or event.

   2. If a correct identification is made, the team receives ten points. If no identification is made within the two-minute time limit, then one point is awarded for every correctly identified word.

   3. Present each team in turn with a different Purim charade. The team with the most points at the end of a designated number of plays wins.

Note: It is suggested that no charade exceed eight words in length. Here are several sample Purim charades.

   1. Esther won the beauty contest of Ahasuerus.

   2. Haman was hung on a tree.

   3. *Hamantachen* look like Haman's three-cornered hat.

   4. On Purim we give gifts to the needy.

INITIALS GAME

Purpose: To challenge one's knowledge of the numerical novelties of Judaism's culture and history

Group: Ages 10 and up

Time: No time limit

Materials: Initial game questions are written on index cards.

Instructions

1. Divide family members into two teams.
2. Each player takes a turn trying to identify a question in an agreed-upon period of time. Each correct answer is awarded one point.
3. The team with the most points wins.

Sample Initial Game Questions and Answers

1. B of E   Book of Esther
2. 10 S of H   Ten Sons of Haman
3. Q E and Q V   Queen Esther and Queen Vashti
4. F M   Five *Megillot*
5. F of E   Fast of Esther

WORD SCRAMBLE

Purpose: To identify scrambled words related to Purim

Group: Ages 10 and up

Time: 20–30 minutes

Materials

1. Words related to Purim on 5- by 7-inch index cards
2. A watch with a second hand

Instructions

1. Divide players into two teams.
2. Hold up the first scrambled word for both teams to review.
3. The first player to raise his or her hand and correctly identify the word receives one point.
4. If no player is able to identify the word after twenty seconds, a new word is displayed to both teams.
5. The team with the most identified words wins.

Sample Words

1. GGRAEGR		GREGGAR
2. HRETES		ESTHER
3. SSAHADAH		HADASSAH
4. GIEMALHL		MEGILLAH
5. ASIREP		PERSIA
6. DAUHES		SEUDAH

HOT POTATO

Purpose: To enjoy Purim songs while manipulating a ball

Group: Ages 5 and up

Time: 15–20 minutes

Materials:
1. Beachball
2. List of Purim Songs

Instructions

1. Ask players to form a circle.
2. Group leader begins to sing a Purim song while a beachball is quickly passed around the circle from hand to hand.
3. When the singing stops, the player holding the ball is eliminated. The ball then continues to rotate as the music starts again to a new song.
4. The game continues. The last person in the circle wins and is given the opportunity to be the singer of the songs in the next round.

HANG HAMAN

Purpose: To identify Purim-related words and themes

Group: Ages 8 and up

Time: 30 minutes

Materials:
1. Flannel board
2. Two sets of the letters of the English alphabet on 3- by 5-inch index cards with flannel backing

3. Black paper strips, 1 inch by 4 inches, with flannel backing

4. A stick figure of Haman, with ten parts of the body, drawn on flannel-backed paper (ten parts = 1 head, 2 arms, 2 legs, 2 eyes, 1 body, 1 nose, 1 mouth)

Instructions

1. Divide players into two teams.

2. Choose a Purim-related word to be identified and place the black paper strips along the bottom of the flannel board (one strip per letter) to indicate the number of letters in the word.

3. The first team plays game one. Ask each player in turn to pick a letter in the word to be identified.

4. Each time a player guesses a correct letter, place that letter in the corresponding blank space on the flannel board. Each wrong guess results in an added part of Haman's body being placed on the flannel board.

5. Players must guess the word before Haman's body is completed. If they do so, they gain one point for their team.

6. The team repeats the procedure with a new word.

7. The team with the most points wins.

BROKEN TELEPHONE

Purpose: To review famous sentences related to the festival of Purim

Group: Ages 5 and up

Time: 30 minutes

Materials

Write Purim-related sentences on index cards. The number of words that are used in the sentences are dependent upon the ages of the children in the family that are playing the game. For children ages ten and under, sentences with ten to twelve words are most suitable. A sample sentence might be: The Jews of Shushan gathered together on the fourteenth of the month of Adar.

Instructions

1. Divide the players into two teams and line them up in single rows.

2. Whisper an identical sentence to the first player on each team. Each player in turn repeats the sentence to the next player on the team, and so on down the line until it reaches the last player.

3. The last player on each team must repeat the sentence.

4. The team with the greatest number of correct words is the winner and receives one point.

5. The last player on each team moves to the first position on the team and the process is repeated.

6. The team with the most points wins.

TO TELL THE TRUTH

Purpose: To enable players to review their knowledge of the Purim story

Group: Ages 10 and up

Time: 10 minutes per play

Materials

1. Costumes for three Purim characters
2. An affidavit that the group leader reads, containing a brief summary of the life of the Purim character to be identified

Instructions

1. Choose three participants to represent a Purim character, for example, Esther. (The group leader decides in advance which participant is the real Esther, the other two being imposters.) The three Esthers dress in costume, and come forward before the group, each in turn identifying herself by stating: "I am Queen Esther."

2. Read the affidavit of Queen Esther and ask the three Queen Esthers to be seated on three straight-back chairs.

3. Choose members of the group to direct questions at the various Queen Esthers (e.g., "What was your other name in the *Megillah* story?" Answer: Hadassah). The Queen Esther imposters are allowed to bluff answers, whereas the real Queen Esther is obliged to tell the truth to the best of her ability.

4. After about five to seven minutes of questioning, ask the questioners to choose the real Queen Esther.

5. The real Queen Esther then stands up in front of the group, and each correct guesser receives one point.

6. At this juncture a new Purim character is chosen and the game replayed.

Note to Group Leader: This game can be played at a Purim party in the home, at a religious school assembly, or as an introduction to the actual *Megillah* reading in the synagogue.

ANAGRAMS

Purpose: To review knowledge of key words related to Purim

Group: Ages dependent upon difficulty of questions

Time: 30 minutes

Materials

1. Index cards (5 inches by 7 inches) with letters of the alphabet written with dark marker. (*Note:* Vowels and certain consonants that tend to repeat during normal usage, e.g., *t* or *m*, ought to be written on several cards.)

2. The group leader has a set of questions related to Purim, with recognized one-word answers appended, for example, "Who was the first queen of Ahasuerus?" Answer: Vashti.

Instructions.

1. Divide players into two teams and give each player several index cards. (The number of cards each player receives is dependent upon the total number of players on a team.)

2. Pose a Purim-related question to the teams.

3. At the word "go," each team must spell out the answer to the question by positioning each player with a lettered index card in an order that will spell out the answer. For example, a possible question to the teams might be "Name the niece of Mordecai." The first person on each team who is in possession of the index card E would line up first, followed by letter S, and so forth, spelling out the correct answer—Esther.

4. The team that answers the question first by spelling out the correct answer wins the point. The team with the most points wins.

PACKING FOR SHUSHAN

Purpose: To enable players to relate their knowledge of Purim to one another.

Group: Ages 10 and up

Time: 15–25 minutes

Materials: None

Instructions

1. One person begins by saying, "I pack my trunk with a Purim costume." The next player, "I pack my trunk with a Purim costume and *greggar*." The third person repeats the first two objects and adds one more, "I pack my trunk with a Purim costume and *greggar* and a mask." Each person repeats all the articles already mentioned and adds a new one.

2. As soon as a player fails to repeat the list correctly, he is eliminated from the game.

3. The game is continued until the contents of the trunk are too numerous to remember.

PURIM LEGENDS

This chapter will introduce you to a variety of Purim legends. They are drawn from a variety of rabbinic sources and will testify to the wildly imaginative thinking of the great leaders of bygone years.

1. When the Jewish people were turned over to the hands of the villain Haman, their very existence as a nation was extremely threatened. This talmudic passage discusses the guilt that was the cause of this grave danger.

Rabbi Simeon the son of Yochai's disciples asked him, "Why did the enemies of Israel of that generation deserve to be annihilated?"

He replied, "Tell me yourselves."

They said, "Because they participated in the feast given by that villain King Ahasuerus."

Rabbi Simeon, the son of Yochai, asked, "If this were the reason, then only the Jews of the capital city of Shushan deserved to die. Why did all of the Jews of the world deserve to die?"

They answered, "You tell us the reason."

He answered, "Because they bowed down to idols during the reign of King Nebuchadnezzar."

Then they asked, "Was partiality shown to them? Why did they deserve such a miracle?"

He replied, "They only bowed down out of fear; therefore, the Holy One, Blessed be He, decreed that they only be chastised and not destroyed. For it is written, For God does not torment wholeheartedly (Lamentations 3:33).

2. Rabbinic opinion states that the ideal repentance does not come as a result of extreme danger but from sincere inner conviction. The Talmud in this selection teaches that God will accept even a lesser form of repentance.

It is written, And the king removed his signet ring (Esther 3:10). Rabbi Aba, the son of Kehana, said, "The removal of King Ahasuerus's signet ring and its delivery into the hands of Haman was more effective than the forty-eight prophets and seven prophetesses who spoke to the people of Israel. These forty-eight prophets and seven prophetesses who spoke to the people of Israel could not convince them to mend their ways, but this one removal of the signet ring was able to accomplish it" (Talmud, *Megillah* 14a).

3. The Talmud also tells of the various expositions of the rabbis on the occasion of the festival of Purim. Here is a sampling of these expositions.

Rabbi Samuel, the son of Nachmeni, began to expound upon the events of Purim: It is written, "Instead of the thorn a fir tree shall arise, and instead of the nettle a myrtle shall arise." (Isaiah 55:13).

The thorn refers to Haman who declared himself an idol, and idols are called thorns . . .

The fir tree refers to Mordecai . . .

The nettle refers to the evil Queen Vashti, the granddaughter of the evil King Nebuchadnezzar, who burned the regal House of our Lord . . .

The myrtle refers to the righteous Esther, who was also known by the name Hadassah, the Hebrew word for "myrtle," as it is written, "And he had brought up Hadassah" (Esther 2:7).

And the verse continues (Esther 2:7), "And it shall be for God for a name" (Isaiah 55:13). This refers to the festival of Purim.

The verse concludes, "For an everlasting sign that shall not be cut off." This refers to the reading of the *Megillah*.

Rabbi Aba, the son of Kehana, began to expound: It is written, "God gives wisdom, knowledge, and joy to a person who is good before Him" (Ecclesiastes 2:26). This refers to Mordecai.

The verse continues (Ecclesiastes 2:26), "And to the sinner God gives the opportunity to gather and to collect." This refers to Haman.

And the verse concludes, "That he may give it to the one who is good before the Lord" (Ecclesiastes 2:26). This refers to Haman's being replaced by Mordecai, as it is written, "And the king removed his signet ring, which he had taken away from Haman, and he gave it to Mordecai, and Esther appointed Mordecai over the house of Haman" (Esther 8:2).

Rabbi Abba, the son of Afron, began to expound: It is written, "And I will place My chair in Eilan, and I will

destroy from there king and princes, by the word of
God" (Jeremiah 49:38). "King" refers to Vashti and
"princes" refers to Haman and his sons.

Rabbi Dimi, the son of Isaac, began to expound: It is
written, "For we were slaves, but our God did not
abandon us in our bondage, and God made us find favor
before the kings of Persia, to provide us with sustenance,
to raise up the House of our God, and to restore its ruins,
and to give us a boundary in Judah and in Jerusalem"
(Ezra 9:9).

When did God make us find favor before the kings of
Persia? In the days of Mordecai and Esther (Talmud,
Megillah 10b).

4. In the following story we learn of Queen Esther's
request to have her memory fixed in the minds of people
for generations to come.

Rabbi Samuel bar Judah said: Esther sent word to the
rabbis, saying: "Fix my memory [in a book] for generations to follow." They sent word back to her, "Such an act
would cause bad feelings against us among the nations
of the world."

Esther replied to them, "But I am already recorded in
the Chronicles of the Kings of Media and Persia" (Talmud, *Megillah* 7a).

5. It was always rabbinic tradition on Purim to drink
enough wine so that one could not distinguish between
the phrases "cursed be Haman" and "blessed be Mordecai." The following talmudic story explains the details.

Rava said, "On Purim it is a person's duty to mellow
himself with wine so that he cannot distinguish between
"cursed be Haman" and "blessed be Mordecai."

Rabbah and Rabbi Zera joined together in a Purim feast. Rabbah became mellow and offered Rabbi Zera so much drink that he passed out. The next day, Rabbah sought mercy and revived him. The following year, when Rabbah said to Rabbi Zera, "Let the master come and we will celebrate Purim together," Rabbi Zera replied, "I regret I cannot come. One cannot expect a miracle on every occasion" (Talmud, *Megillah* 7a).

6. A significant amount of legendary material relates to the kind of wood that was chosen in order for Haman to fashion the gallows upon which the Jews would die. Here is an exposition of these deliberations.

Of what kind of tree were the gallows fashioned? Our sages said: When he came to make it ready, God called all of the trees at the time of creation together and said, "Which will make an offer to be used to hang this man?"

The fig tree said, "I will offer myself, for from me do the Israelites bring first fruits. Furthermore, Israel is also compared to a first ripe fruit, as it is written, 'I saw your fathers as the first ripe fruit in the fig tree at her first season'" (Hosea 9:10).

Then the vine said, "I offer myself, since Israel is compared to me, as it is written, 'You did pluck up a vine out of Egypt'" (Psalms 80:9).

The pomegranate said, "I offer myself, since Israel is compared to me, as it is written, 'Your temples are like a pomegranate split open'" (Song of Songs 4:3).

Then the nut tree said, "I offer myself, because Israel is likened to me, as it is written, 'I went down into the garden of nuts'" (Song of Songs 6:11).

The citron said, "I offer myself because Israel takes my fruit for ritual purposes, as it is written, 'And you shall take for yourself on the first day the fruit of goodly trees'" (Leviticus 23:40).

The myrtle said, "I offer myself, because Israel is compared to me, as it is written, 'And he stood among the myrtles that were in the bottom'" (Zechariah 1:8).

The olive tree said, "I offer myself, since Israel is compared to me, as it is written, 'The Lord called your name a leafy olive tree, fair with goodly fruit'" (Jeremiah 11:16).

The apple tree said, "I offer myself, because Israel is compared to me, as it is written, 'As an apple tree among the trees of the wood, so is my beloved among the sons' (Song of Songs 2:3), and it also says, 'And the smell of your countenance is like apples'" (Song of Songs 7:9).

The palm tree said, "I offer myself, because Israel is likened to me, as it is written, 'Thus your stature is like a palm tree'" (Song of Songs 7:8).

The acacia and fir trees said, "We offer ourselves because the tabernacle and the Temple were built from our wood."

The cedar and the palm tree said, "We offer ourselves, because we are compared to the righteous, as it is written, 'The righteous shall grow like the palm tree and like a mighty cedar in Lebanon'" (Psalms 92:13).

The willow said, "I offer myself, because Israel is compared to me, as it is written, 'They shall spring up . . . as willows by the watercourses' (Isaiah 44:4) and they also use me for the ceremony of the four species of the *lulav*."

Then the thorn said to the Holy One, Blessed be He: "King of the Universe, I who have no claim to make offer myself, that this unclean person may be hanged on me, because my name is thorn and he is a prickly thorn, and it is only proper that one thorn should be hanged upon another thorn."

So they found one of these and they made the gallows. When they brought it to him, he set it up at the entrance of his house and he measured himself on it to show his servants how Mordecai ought to be hanged on it. A Heavenly Voice answered him: "For you is the tree fitting. The tree has been made ready for you from the beginning of the final judgment."

The Babylonian teachers asked, "How do we know that Haman is derived from the Torah? Because it is written *hamin ha'etz*—'hast you'—of the tree" (Genesis 3:3) (*Esther Rabbah* 9:2).

7. Esther was known for her acts of heroism in the Scroll of Esther. When she realizes that it is she who may have the best opportunity to defeat the evil Haman, she begins to design a plan of attack. One of her earliest decisions was to invite King Ahasuerus and Haman to dine with her. The Talmud elaborates upon her plot in much detail.

Our rabbis have taught: Why did Esther see fit to invite Haman to dine?

Rabbi Elazar says: "She prepared a snare with which to entrap, as it is written, 'Let their table be as a snare before them'" (Psalms 69:23).

Rabbi Joshua says: "She had learned this method of overcoming her foes in her own father's house. For it is written, 'If your enemy is hungry, feed him bread; if he is thirsty, give him some water to drink, for you will be heaping burning coals upon his head, and God will repay you'" (Proverbs 25:21–22). In another variant reading, the verse says that God will turn him over to you.

Rabbi Meir says, "Esther did so in order to give Haman a false sense of security, thus preventing him from revolting against the king."

Rabbi Judah said, "She did so to hide the fact that she was Jewish."

Rabbi Nechemiah says, "Esther was afraid that the Jews would think that they did not have to pray for mercy since one of their own was the king's wife [i.e., Esther]. Therefore, she invited Haman to her house to give the Jews the false impression that she was allied with Haman and to induce them to pray to God."

Rabbi Jose says, "Esther wanted Haman to be in her company often, because this would increase the opportunity of entrapping him."

Rabbi Simeon, the son of Menasia, says, "Esther did so hoping that God would take note of her dire situation and perform miracles for the Jews."

Rabbi Joshua, the son of Karcha, says, "Esther wanted to show a friendly interest in Haman so that King Ahasuerus would put both Haman and her to death."

Rabbi Gamaliel said: "Ahasuerus was a very fickle-minded king."

Rabbi Gamaliel then said, "After all is said and done, we still need the explanation of Rabbi Elazar from Moda."

It was taught: Rabbi Elazar from Moda says, "Esther wanted to arouse the jealousy of the king against Haman as well as the jealousy of all of the other ministers she had not invited."

Rabba quoted: "Pride goes before ruin" (Proverbs 16:18).

Abaye and Rabba both quoted: "When they are

heated, I will set out their drink, and I will get them drunk so that they will fall unconscious, and they shall not awaken, declares God."

Rabba, the son of Avuha, met the prophet Elijah and asked him, "What was the real reason for Esther inviting the king and Haman to dine with her?"

Elijah replied, "Her reasons included all of those put forth by the *tannaim* and *amoraim*" (Talmud, *Megillah* 15b).

8. The Book of Esther is one of only two books of the Bible (the other is the Song of Songs) that does not have a direct reference to God. However, the ancient rabbis deemed it important that the Scroll of Esther was not simply a chronicle of events that occurred in Shushan but rather that the plot of the book unfolded through Divine inspiration. Here is the way that the Talmud tells it:

Rabbi Eliezer says: "The Book of Esther was composed under the inspiration of the holy spirit. For it is written, "And Haman thought to himself . . .'" (Esther 6:6).

Rabbi Akiva says, "The Book of Esther was written with the holy spirit. For it is written, 'And Esther found favor in the eyes of all who saw her'" (Esther 2:15).

Rabbi Meir says, "Esther was composed under the inspiration of the holy spirit, as it says, 'And the thing became known to Mordecai.'"

Rabbi Jose, the son of Durmaskis, says, "The Book of Esther was written under the inspiration of the holy spirit. For it is written, 'But on the spoil they laid not their hands'" (Esther 9:10).

Rabbi Samuel said, "Had I been there, I would have

given a superior proof to all, namely, that it says 'they confirmed and took upon them,' which means that they confirmed in heaven what they took upon themselves below" (Talmud, *Megillah* 7a).

9. The ancient rabbis established the holiday of Purim as a day of rejoicing and of sending presents and giving gifts to poor people. Today it is common for people to share food baskets with each other and also donate food on Purim to food shelters and pantries. The Talmud amplifies the details of these presents and gifts on Purim.

Rabbi Joseph taught, "And sending portions to one another" means two portions to one person.

"And gifts to the poor." This verse means two gifts to two persons.

Rabbi Judah Nesiah sent to R. Oshaia the leg of a third-born calf and a barrel of wine. He sent him back word saying, "You have fulfilled in our person, master, the words of the verse 'and sending portions to one another.'"

Rabbah sent to Mari, the son of Mar by Abaye, a sackful of dates and a cupful of roasted ears of corn. Abaye said to him, "Mari will now say, 'If a countryman becomes a king, he does not take his basket off his neck' [an indication of a lowly gift]." Mari sent Rabbah back a sackful of ginger and a cup full of longstalked pepper. Abaye said, "Now Rabbah will say I sent him sweet and he sent me bitter."

Abaye said, "When I went out of Rabbah's house I was already sated, but when I reached the other place, they placed before me sixty dishes of various prepared foods and I ate parts of these sixty dishes. The last dish

contained a roast that was so good that I ate all of it, and
I even wanted to eat the dish itself! This bears out the
popular saying that a poor person is so hungry and does
not know it, or the other saying that there is always room
for sweet things. Abaye, the son of Abin, and Rabbi
Hananiah, the son of Abin, used to exchange their Purim
meals with one another" (Talmud, *Megillah* 7a).

10. The name Mordecai is said to be derived from a
Persian word meaning "warlike." The name Hadassah,
Esther's alternate name in the Scroll of Esther, is said to
be derived from the Hebrew *hadas* meaning "a myrtle
sprig." In the following deliberations these names and
their meanings are further elaborated.

As myrrh (*mor*) is the foremost of spices, so *Mor*decai
was the foremost of the righteous of his generation
(*Esther Rabbah* 2:5).

Mordecai raised Esther. She had been named Hadassah (myrtle) because as the myrtle spreads its fragrance,
so she spread her good works throughout all of the land.
She was also called Hadassah because righteous people
are compared to myrtle, like Hananiah, Mishael, and
Azariah, of whom it is written, "And he stood among the
myrtle trees" (Zechariah 1:8).

She was also named Hadassah because just as the
myrtle does not wither in summer or winter, so the
righteous do not die but have a share both in this world
and in the world to come. Esther always remained the
same in her youth and never once stopped from per-
forming good deeds. She was called Esther because she
was like the planet Venus, which in Greek is Astara (2
Targum 2:6, 7).

11. A most interesting legend relates to the fact that when Esther was cut off from communication with the Jews, the rabbis felt that she would be in danger of forgetting the very essence of the Sabbath, and even the day on which the Sabbath fell. The following tale describes the elaborate mechanism by which she was able to remember the Sabbath day.

> Esther was cut off from all communication and discourse with her fellow Jews. She was now in great danger of forgetting the day on which the Sabbath arrived. She then adopted a way of giving her seven attendants unusual names, in order for her to track the course of time during the week. The first attendant she called Hulta—"Workaday"—and she was with Esther on Sundays. On Mondays, Esther was served by Rokita, to remind her of *Rakiah*—Firmament, which was created by God on the second day of creation of the world. Genunita—"Garden"—was the name of Tuesday's attendant, because on the third day God created the plants and vegetation of the world.
>
> On Wednesday, God made the luminaries to shed their lights on the world. Esther's attendant this day was Nehorita—"Luminous." On Thursday, the maid's name was Ruhshita—"Movement," for on this day animated beings were created. On Friday, the day on which the beasts were created, Esther called her maid Hurfita—"Little Ewelamb." Finally, on the seventh day, Esther's attendant received the name Regoita—"Rest." In this way Esther was able to remember the Sabbath day as each week passed by (1 *Targum* 2:9).

12. One important heroic act in the Book of Esther was Mordecai's refusal to bow down to the evil Haman.

The following tale provides more details about this extremely brave act.

> The king commanded that all the Jewish people should bow down and show reverence to Haman. What did Haman then decide to do? He made for himself an image of an old idol and had it embroidered upon his dress, above his heart, so that all who bowed to Haman also bowed down to the idol that he made. Seeing this, Mordecai did not consent to bow down to the idol, as it is written, "But Mordecai did not bow down" (Esther 3:2) (*Pirke de Rabbi Eliezer* 50).

13. A most interesting tale relates to the inability of King Ahasuerus to sleep (Esther 6:1) after the gallows had been prepared by Haman. In this astounding tale we see the imagination of the rabbis as even Moses the Prophet makes an appearance in an attempt to arouse the compassion of God.

> Having created the gallows, Haman went to Mordecai, whom he found in the house of study with the school-children sitting before him with sackcloth, studying the Torah and crying. Haman counted them and found twenty-two thousand children. He put iron chains on them and set guards over them. Then he said, "Tomorrow I will kill the children first, and then I will hang Mordecai."
>
> Their mothers brought them water and food to eat and said, "Children, eat and drink before you die tomorrow." Immediately, the children put their hands on their books and swore by Mordecai's life that they would not eat or drink, but rather die while fasting. They cried incessantly until their crying reached the heavens and the Holy One,

Blessed be He, heard their weeping at the second hour
of the night. At that moment God's compassion was
aroused, and God arose from the Throne of Judgment
and sat on the Throne of Mercy and said: "What is this
loud noise that I hear as the bellowing of kids and
lambs?"

It was then that Moses our teacher stood before the
Holy One, Blessed be He, and said: "Master of the Universe, they are neither kids nor lambs, but the little ones
of Your people who have been fasting now for three days
and three nights, and tomorrow they will be slaughtered
by the enemy." At that very moment the Holy One,
Blessed be He, took the letters containing their impending doom, which were signed with a clay seal, and tore
them and brought dread upon Ahasuerus that night, as it
is written, "During the night the king was disturbed . . ."
(Esther 6:1) (*Esther Rabbah* 9:4).

14. It has always appeared in the Book of Esther that
Esther acts without the need for a morale boost by her
Uncle Mordecai. It is also reasonable to assume (putting
ourselves in Esther's shoes) that Esther might easily have
believed that she would not have to worry about any
danger to her own life because of her status in the king's
court. The following tale dispels this myth by presenting
the charge of Mordecai to his niece Esther.

Mordecai addressed Esther with this statement: "You
might imagine that you are safe [because she was, of
course, the queen of Shushan] and that you need not
pray for Israel. Know, however, that if only a foot of one
single Jew is injured, don't think that you, of all Jews, will
escape. Therefore, go and pray to your heavenly Father

on behalf of the people of Israel. God who did justice for the first generation will also do justice to those who come after them. Is Haman so strong that we should fear him? Is he really stronger than his ancestor Amalek, who came against the Israelites, but whom God removed from the world? Therefore, do not withhold your prayer, nor your lips for asking mercy of the Source of all creation. For the sake of the righteous of our ancestors, Israel has been delivered. God will now also deliver them from our enemies.

O Esther, do not think that you shall be saved in the house of the king. For if you shall be silent at this time, God will cause redemption to spring up for the Israelites from another place, but you and your father's house will perish. And who knows whether you have not come to the kingdom because of the sins of your father's house" (2 *Targum* 4:13–14).

15. The following *midrash* is a rabbinic attempt to help solve the theological difficulty of the lack of divine intervention in the Book of Esther.

When the wicked Haman said to King Ahasuerus: "Come, let us exterminate Israel," Ahasuerus replied: "You cannot triumph over them since their God will not entirely abandon them. See what He did to kings who came before us and who laid hands upon them and who were much stronger than we were. Whoever will come against them to destroy them and whoever plots against them will be destroyed. How much more so then we who are not equal to those others. Let me hear no more of this."

In spite of all of this the wicked Haman pressed this upon Ahasuerus on every occasion, and tried to per-

suade him to oppress Israel. Finally Ahasuerus said to
him, "Since you are so persistent, let us consult the wise
men of the nations." When they all gathered before him
he said, "Is it your desire that we destroy the nation?"
They all replied with one voice: "Who is he, and where
is he, that dost presume in his heart to do so, (Esther 7:5)
and wishes to cast lots for such a matter? For if you
destroy Israel, the world cannot exist, for it stands only
through the merit of the Law which was given to
Israel. . ." (*Esther Rabbah* 7:13).

16. King Ahasuerus was the King of Shushan and one
of the main characters in the Book of Esther. The
following *midrash* explains the derivation of his most
unusual name.

Rabbi Joshua, the son of Karchas, said: He was called
Ahasuerus because he made the face of Israel black [in
Hebrew, *bichshir*] like the sides of a pot.

Rabbi Berekiah said: Because he made the head of
Israel ache [in Hebrew, *bichish rosh*] with fasting and all
kinds of affliction.

Rabbi Levi said: Because he made them drink gall [in
Hebrew, *bishkah rosh*] and wormwood.

Rabbi Judah said: Because he sought to uproot Israel
from its foundation.

Rabbi Tachalifa, the son of Bar Channa, said: Because
he was the brother of the head [in Hebrew, *achiv shel
rosh*], the brother of Nebuchadnezzar. . . (*Esther Rabbah* 1:1).

17. The following *midrash* elaborates on the verse
from the Book of Esther: "And Mordecai told him [i.e.,
Hatach] all that happened." It occurred after Mordecai

had learned that Haman was going to exterminate all of the Jews.

> Mordecai told him that which happened to him in a dream in which he dreamt the following: In the second year of King Ahasuerus he saw, and behold there was a great quaking, and much confusion all over the earth, and fear came upon all of the inhabitants. Two dragons raised a cry against one another and prepared for a fight, and all the nations of the earth fled when they heard their voice. Among them was one small nation, and all the nations rose against that small nation to strike out its remembrance from the earth. On that very day the earth was covered with darkness, and that small nation was in great distress and cried to God. The dragons fought with fierce anger and no one parted them. Then Mordecai beheld that a small stream of water passed between these two dragons and put an end to their fighting. The stream grew and became a river in flood like the sea and it overflowed the earth. And he saw the sun rise over all of the earth and light over the world. And the small nation was exalted and the lofty were brought low, and there was truth and peace upon earth. From that day onward Mordecai kept in mind the dream which he had dreamed, and when Haman angered him he said to Esther by her messenger, "Here is the dream which I related to you in your childhood. Rise and pray for mercy from God and come before the king and pray for your people and your kindred" (*Esther Rabbah* 8:5).

18. In Chapter 4 of the Book of Esther, Esther tells Mordecai to go and assemble all of Shushan's Jews and proclaim a fast. The text then proceeds to tell us that "Mordecai did all that Esther had commanded him to

do." The following *midrash* details that which Mordecai did on behalf of the Jewish people.

Mordecai spent the Passover festival in fasting on account of the calamity. He prayed to God and said: "It is fully known that it was not from pride of heart that I decided not to bow down to Haman, but through fear of You. If I was in fear of You, O God, lest I should assign Your honor to flesh and blood, and I was not willing to bow down to anyone else besides you. For who am I that I should not bow down to Haman for the salvation of Your people. For that I would even kiss his shoelace. Now therefore, O God, deliver us, we pray, from his hand and let him fall into the pit which he has dug and let him be trapped in the snare which he has hidden for the feet of Your saints, and let this sinner know that You have not forgotten the promise which You have made to us: 'Yet for all that, when you are in the land of their enemies, I will not reject them, neither will I abhor them, to totally destroy them, and to break My covenant with them. For I am their God'" (Leviticus 14:44).

What did Mordecai then do? He collected all of the schoolchildren and kept them without bread and water and put sackcloth on them and made them sit among the ashes . . . At the same time Esther was frightened of the impending evil that threatened Israel, and she took off her royal garments and loosened the hair of her head and filled with it dust and ashes and afflicted herself by fasting and fell on her face before God. And she prayed and said, "O God of Israel Who is Ruler from of old and Creator of the world, help Your handmaid who has been left an orphan without a father or mother, and is like a poor woman begging from house to house. So I pray for Your grace from one window to another in the palace of

Ahasuerus. O God, grant success to your humble handmaid here and deliver the sheep of Your pasture from
these enemies who have risen against us. . ." (*Esther
Rabbah* 8:6).

19. In chapter 5:1, Esther comes to the king's court
without being called. This, of course, is a violation and
Esther's life is now greatly endangered. The following
midrash uses the intervention of God in order to explain
how Esther is able to overcome a dangerous situation.

> Then Esther came to the inner court facing the king
> and stood before him. The king was sitting on his royal
> throne in a gold robe on which were precious stones,
> and when he lifted up his eyes he saw Esther standing in
> front of him. He was very angry because she had broken
> his law, having come before him unannounced.
> Then Esther lifted up her eyes and saw the king's face,
> and his eyes were filled with fire and he was angry in his
> heart. And when Esther realized how angry he was, she
> was overcome with fear and her heart sank. She placed
> her hand on her maiden who was supporting her right
> hand.
> But God had mercy on His people, and took cogni-
> zance of the orphan who trusted in Him and He gave her
> grace in the eyes of the king, investing her with a
> renewed beauty and allure.
> Then the king quickly rose from his throne and ran to
> Esther. Embracing and kissing her, he said, "Esther, my
> queen, why are you trembling? For the law which we
> have laid down does not apply to you, since you are my
> beloved and companion." He also asked her, "Why
> when I saw you did you not speak to me?"

Esther answered, "My lord the king, when I saw you I was overcome by your high dignity" (*Esther Rabbah* 9:1).

20. The rabbis asked the following question: "Why was Israel of that generation deemed to be deserving of extermination?" The following is one rabbinic answer.

His students asked Rabbi Simeon ben Yochai: Why was the Israel of that particular generation deemed to deserve annihilation? He said to them: "You tell me."

They replied, "Because Israel relished the feast of that wicked one."

He then said, "If so, the Jews in Susa should have also been condemned to die, but not those in the rest of the world."

They then said, "You tell us, then."

He said, "Because they bowed down to graven images."

Then they asked, "Was there a show of favor toward them on God's part in this matter?

He answered, "No! Since they only pretended to pray to graven images, God only pretended that He was about to exterminate them" (Talmud, *Megillah* 12a).

21. The Book of Esther (1:6) describes the couches in the King's palace as being of gold and silver. The following tale explains how people of different stations were allowed to sit on them.

It was taught that Rabbi Judah said, "The person who was rated worthy of silver was invited to sit on a silver couch, while the one who was rated worthy of gold was asked to recline on a gold couch."

Rabbi Nehemiah argued, "Showing this kind of favor-
itism would surely have stirred up resentment and ill
feelings at the feast. Rather, what the verse really means
is that all of the couches were made of silver, and only
their legs were made of gold. . ." (Talmud, *Megillah*
12a).

22. The following *midrash* elaborates upon the grievance that two of the king's chamberlains, Bigthan and
Teresh, were said to have in the Book of Esther 2:21.

What brought on the grievance? Rabbi Levi said,
"Bigthan and Teresh were Tarseans, and both sat in the
king's gate. But the king removed them and substituted
Mordecai in their place. It was then that they felt that
they had a grievance. What did they then decide to do?
They said, "Let's put poison in the king's bowl, so that
the king will die and everybody will say, 'When Bigthan
and Teresh used to guard the king, all was well, but now
that a Jew was substituted in their place, the king is
murdered.'"
They were both standing talking of their scheme in
the Tarsean language, not knowing that Mordecai was
one of those who had sat in the chamber of hewn stone
and therefore knew the seventy languages of the world
(Talmud, *Megillah* 13b).

23. This tale provides us with the reason for Haman's
promotion (mentioned in the Book of Esther 3:1).

Rabbi Levi said, "Haman was promoted only for his
downfall. Why then was it necessary to promote him?
The answer will now be provided by the parable of a
common soldier who cursed the king's son. The king

said, 'If I put this rogue to death, everybody will say, "The king has executed a common soldier." I will first promote him, then I will kill him.'"

So he made him a tribune, and then a general, and subsequently beheaded him. Likewise, the Holy One said, "Should Haman be put to death when he sank so low as to advise Ahasuerus to stop the building of the Temple, no one will know who he is. Let him therefore be promoted and then be hanged."

So "he first set his seat above the princes" (Esther 3:1) and after that they hanged Haman (Esther 7:10). This shows how God's enemies become great only as a prelude to their downfall. And thus the Bible says (Psalms 92:8), Though the wicked sprout, they are like grass. What follows at the end of this verse? "Only that they may be destroyed forever. . ." (*Esther Rabbah* 7:2).

24. Haman's wickedness permeates the Book of Esther. Here is a tale elaborating on his wickedness and comparing it to a certain kind of bird.

To what may the wicked Haman be compared? To a bird that made its nest at the edge of the sea, only to have it swept away when the tide was high. What did the bird do? It took water into its beak and proceeded to pour it over dry land, then it took sand from the dry land and dropped it into the sea.

Its companion then came by and asked, "What are you doing, and why are you working so hard?"

To which the bird answered, "I will not leave from this place until I turn the sea into dry land and the dry land into the sea."

Its companion then replied, "You are a big fool! After

all of this effort, what do you think that you can accomplish?"

So, too, the Holy One said to the wicked Haman: "You are the biggest fool in the world. I said that I would destroy Israel, and found," if one dare ascribe such words to God, "that I could not." As the Bible says, "God intended to destroy them, but then Moses, God's chosen one, stood before Him in the breach. . ." (*Esther Rabbah* 7:10).

PURIM IN THE SHORT STORY

1. GOOD PURIM, GOOD PURIM!!

Moshele, the water carrier, was a meek, downtrodden man who barely earned enough from his labors to feed his large family. One Purim he went to the home of his rebbe, Rabbi Israel, the Maggid of Kozenitz, to wish him a Good Purim. Head bowed, he slunk into the house and mumbled, "Good Purim," in a dispirited voice.

The Maggid upbraided him sharply, saying, "Moshele, how can you greet me with such a feeble 'Good Purim'? And where are your *shalakh manos* for today?"

"Rabbi," protested Moshele, "I owe the grocer money. I owe the baker money, and the tailor and the shoe-maker. Where could I get enough money to buy *shalakh manos* for you?"

"Moshele," smiled the rabbi. "When you learn to say 'Good Purim,' everything will come your way. Then you will return here with proper *shalakh manos*."

Moshele left the rabbi's house more dejected than before. Not only did he have a mountain of debts he could not pay, but even his rebbe had turned him away because of his poverty.

Hoping to beg one more ruble of credit, Moshele went to the grocery store. But as soon as he walked in the door, the grocer said to him, "Ah, Moshele, maybe you've come to pay me some of the money you owe me?"

Moshele's heart sank. Then he remembered the Maggid's words. With his head held high, he said cheerfully "Today is Purim, grocer! Today there is no evil in the world. Good Purim!"

The astonished grocer forgot all about Moshele's overdue bills and gave him enough cakes, honey, and wine for his *shalakh manos* basket. Overjoyed, Moshele ran to the Maggid's house and gave him the basket.

"Good, Moshele!" smiled the Maggid. "I see that you are learning to say, 'Good Purim!' Don't you know that today is a wonderful day? Haman and Amalek have been defeated!"

Moshele returned to the grocer and greeted him with another confident "Good Purim!" Then he asked for groceries to provide for his family's Purim *seudah*. The grocer filled his basket with fish, *hallah*, honey, cakes, and wine.

"Thank you!" shouted Moshele as he left the store! "Just put it on my bill. Today is a wonderful day! Our enemies have been defeated! Good Purim!!"

Next he went to the tailor, whose shop he had not entered in ten years.

"Good Purim, tailor!" he cried joyfully as he walked through the door. The tailor dropped his needle and thread in surprise. What was Moshele doing here? Had he suddenly inherited a fortune?

"I want you to make clothes for my entire family," said

Moshele. "A new dress for my beloved wife, a new coat for me, and pretty things for all the children."

"Moshele," said the astonished tailor, "the last time you came in here—ten years ago—you bought a suit, and you still owe me money for it!"

"But today is Purim!" said Moshele. "Let's rejoice, for wicked Haman has been defeated! Good Purim!"

"Good Purim to you, Moshele!" answered the bewildered tailor, and he set to work measuring Moshele for a new coat. Then he went to the back of his shop and brought back a tower of boxes. "For your wife and children," he said, handing the boxes to Moshele.

"Just put it on my bill," said Moshele, walking out the door. "Good Purim!"

Then Moshele went home and handed his astonished wife all the packages he was carrying. "Good Purim, dear wife!" he cried. "Stand tall and proud, children! For today is Purim! There is no more evil in the world, for our enemies have been defeated. Say 'Good Purim' with joy in your hearts!"

"Good Purim, Papa!" the children cried, and their hearts did indeed dance with joy.

Then Moshele went to the bank. He marched up to the window and, in a confident voice, said to the teller, "I wish to speak to the manager!"

The startled teller scurried off and soon returned with the manager.

"What seems to be the problem?" asked the manager.

"I am Moshele, the water carrier," said Moshele, "but I do not wish to remain a water carrier all my life. I want a loan so that I can start my own business. Today is

Purim! We have triumphed over our enemies. Good Purim!"

Impressed by Moshele's confidence, the banker lent him the money he needed to start a business. In a short time, Moshele became a successful merchant and repaid all his debts. The wealthier he became, the more he gave to the poor and oppressed in Kozenitz.

And every Purim the Maggid sent all his followers to Moshele's house to learn how to say "Good Purim! Good Purim!"

2. PURIM PLAYER

by M. Dluznowsky

Everyone knew Simon the Redhead. Simon was an orphan. At the age of eight he had to look out for himself. To earn his living, he did jobs. He worked at the bakery, helped the glazier with the window panes, stretched skins in the tannery, watered the coachman's horses. He was busy all year round.

But there was one day of the year when Simon the Redhead forgot about all his chores and enjoyed a holiday. That day was Purim.

On Purim he was just like the other boys on the street. All the children wore masks and no one recognized the other. With masked faces, all were alike—the rich and the poor. You couldn't tell the difference between Simon the Redhead and Berel, the miller's son. You would not even know which was Meyer, the only son of the rich manufacturer who lived in the village.

However, the truth is that even on Purim, Simon had a complaint.

The boys who dressed as Purim players always insisted that Simon play the part of Haman. At first, Simon readily played the role of the villain. But after a few years he rebelled.

"I want to play Mordecai once," he said.

"Listen to him!" the others jeered. "He thinks we'll let *him* play Mordecai. If you don't want the part, we'll get another Haman."

Simon's face was beet-red. Trembling with anger, he cried out:

"I'm Haman every year. Why doesn't Meyer or David or somebody else play the part? It's Purim, isn't it? It's just make believe!"

Nothing helped. The boys were angry. They found another Haman and Simon was left out of the play.

That Purim Simon was alone. But his mind was made up. He would show them! He would dress as Mordecai, go from house to house, sing a Purim song, make a Purim speech, and act the part so well that everyone would recognize him as Mordecai the Righteous.

But he needed a beard, a long robe, a sash. He had none of these things, and soon the day was almost over. Families were already sitting down to their Purim feast, all dressed in holiday finery. The Purim players were gathering in groups, wearing costumes and masks, some in their parents' old clothes.

Desperately, Simon ran to Reuben, the baker, who smeared his chin, his lips, and cheeks with soot and ashes from the oven. He turned his hat and tattered coat around, back to front, and ran out into the street ready to play Mordecai.

Unasked and uninvited, he came into homes all by

himself—a Mordecai without a Haman, without a king, even without a royal guard. But wherever he went, he acted his part bravely, and people applauded and filled his pockets with jingling coins.

The boys on the street soon learned about Simon's success. The very next day, they promised him that next Purim they would gladly let him play Mordecai.

That night Simon slept a sweet sleep. He had been a real hero for once in his life.

3. THE SOUND OF THE *GREGGARS*

by Robert Garvey

This year Gabriel had the honor of reading the *Megillah*.

The other angels listened to his sweet voice, nodding and sometimes humming along, for they loved every word of the beautiful old story of Esther. When Gabriel read the name "Haman," however, there was a noise like a thunderclap that toppled Gabriel off his chair and brought all the other angels to their feet.

Where had the noise come from? Surely, there are no *greggars* in heaven. In fact, there are no noise-makers of any kind. Even the heavenly orchestra, which is easily the largest in the universe, has no snaredrums, kettle-drums, cymbals, or other claptrap noisemakers.

And so the questioning eyes of the angels turned to the Throne of the Most High.

"Do you not know?" the Lord said.

But none of the angels could imagine where the noise had come from.

Gabriel went on with the reading. But when he pronounced the word "Haman" again, a terrifying roar shook the universe.

"How disturbing!" several angels said, quite nervous. And Archangel Gabriel said, "It can't be a heavenly creature who is doing this. It must be someone from below—someone who is different from us."

And so Elijah—who was a kind of Heavenly Messenger—was sent out to see where the noise was coming from.

Flying smoothly, he took a turn around Saturn and Neptune and even Venus and Mars. But all was peaceful there as the planets moved quietly around the sun and their moons moved quietly around them.

Elijah shook his head sadly. I guess it's earth again, he thought. He then checked on the dozen or so thunderstorms breaking out around the equator. But those weren't loud enough to reach Heaven.

And so he began a careful search. He checked every house of every street of every town and village until he came to a somewhat noisy synagogue.

Inside, the synagogue was crowded with men and women and mostly with children. A man up front was reading the *Megillah*, and every time the name "Haman" was read, the children swung their *greggars*. Elijah knew this was an old practice on Earth.

But the sound of the *greggars* was not remarkably loud. Not as all as loud as guns or thunderbolts. The windows didn't even rattle. Only the children kept swinging their *greggars* long after the name "Haman" was read, so that the *shammash* had to hold up his hand and tell them to stop or the reading would not go on.

"Good Purim to you, stranger!" a man said to Elijah with a chuckle. "Did you ever hear such fun-makers? Once these silly kids get a *greggar* in their hands they can't stop them!"

"Oh, dear, they are so wild this year," an older man said, frowning over his glasses. "And the rabbi gave them such a nice sermon, such a nice sermon. About being different, you know." And he whispered to Elijah: "You know? He told them all about Haman—how he couldn't bear people being different from himself. And so he tried to destroy these people who were different. Now isn't that a nice sermon? Isn't it? But in one ear and out the other with these children. Oh, they listened quietly while the rabbi spoke. But now see how wild they are. If only they were different! Well, I do hope you will excuse us, stranger. Our synagogue is usually an orderly place, it is."

Elijah looked around. Some of the children were giggling and whirling their *greggars* just for the fun, but some of them were turning their *greggars* as if their lives depended on it! Elijah asked one or two of these children what they were doing, but all they would say was, "Oh, we're drowning out Haman!"

Elijah stroked his beard. He was sure that these were the noises that were reaching Heaven, but he did not know why. So he concentrated very hard until he could see right into the minds and hearts of the children. And this is what he found out.

The little girl in the blue dress, swinging her *greggar* with all her might, was thinking: I'm drowning out the voice of the man who told me not to play with my friend because she has a skin of a different color of mine.

The boy whirling his *greggar* breathlessly had this on his mind: I am drowning out the voice of the woman who told me not to go to school with my friend because his skin is a different color from mine.

And the little boy tearfully shaking his *greggar* was thinking: Just because I'm littler than him, the big bully won't let me play in the basketball game. I'm drowning out what he said to me.

And still other children were making noises to drown out what people said about other people because they were different.

Elijah stopped concentrating and smiled. He knew there was nothing anybody could do to stop these noises from breaking the quiet in Heaven.

But he hoped that the people on Earth would just listen a little to the *greggar* sounds and know what was on the minds and hearts of their children.

4. THE PURIM ROSE

by Claudine Naar

Esther isn't very pleased with Purim this year. Somehow, it isn't as much fun as usual, and she makes a sour face to show her annoyance.

Outwardly, everything seems the same as last year. The table is laden with *Hamantachen* and other cakes. Esther's friends at the party are all wearing beautiful costumes. And at the synagogue, the noise was ear-shattering when Haman's name was read in the *Megillah*.

Back home now, Esther sighs, even though she is wearing a long satin robe and has a glittering crown perched on her head. She remembers that her name is the same as that of the heroine of Purim: you might say that in a way Purim is dedicated to her own small self. Ah, if only she could be a heroine. Then she could help her people escape from all sorts of perils and she could destroy all the Hamans in the world! And maybe God, noticing her youth, would not make her fast for three days as the real Queen Esther did.

The laughter and hubbub of the party shatters her golden daydream. She'd better pay attention to her guests! She smiles as her father lovingly calls her "my little queen," and she curtseys when her friends address her as "Your Majesty." Every mirror reflects her regal image. How sad it is that her younger sister must bear the oh-so ordinary name of Annette!

All in all, Esther really cannot decide why it is that she feels so gloomy. Everything is moving smoothly and the party seems to be a huge success.

Finally, she is forced to face the real explanation of her sadness—Gerard is not here,

And just who is Gerard? Why . . . no one in particular. But that isn't quite true either; he is one of her many friends. Esther meets him at the Champs de Mars every Thursday. Of course she also meets Albert, George, Lily, and Jacqueline. All are her playmates, but perhaps she does have a preference for Gerard. He seems to like her a lot, too. Once he even dared ask her to make a solemn pledge that she would promise to marry no one but him when they grew up. Esther had been quite shocked. Hadn't Mother taught her never to make an oath? And besides, didn't she like Albert and George, too?

Gerard had been very annoyed when Esther refused to tell him why she hesitated. "Gerard," she had said, "I will give you my answer next week." But Thursday came and Gerard seemed to forget all about his marriage plans.

They had both been seated on a bench in the Champs de Mars. They were breathless from running and shouting and laughing. Maybe Gerard was teasing Esther more than usual, too, and he kept making fun of the way she caught the ball when it was thrown to her. When she had had just about enough, she turned and gave him a good wallop across the face. Let's see what he will say to that, she thought. But he didn't say a word. He just picked himself up and marched off, leaving little Esther with a tingling hand and a red face.

And now it was Purim, and Mama, as was her yearly custom, had invited all the children to a Purim party. Everybody came in costume—one was a Turkish prince, another a pastry cook, a third was a devil. Everybody was there. Except Gerard.

Hmph! It's just as well, thought Esther. She would not have spoken to him anyway. What's more, she never wants to see him again. Never! Suddenly a memory of last Purim sneaks into her thoughts. A letter had arrived in the morning mail addressed to her. Then someone noticed a word written awkwardly on the lower left corner of the envelope: "Personal." Papa, Mama, and Annette had burst out laughing. Blushing, Esther opened her letter. Slowly she read: "Today's festival really belongs to you, Esther, so I am sending you all my love and a great big kiss."

But that was last year. Now the hands of the clock move on, and Esther admits that deep in her heart she had been expecting Gerard all along. The party is breaking up. One after another Esther's friends say goodbye. The house is empty now. Only cake crumbs on the table, chairs strewn helter-skelter, and a very unhappy little girl. How could Gerard have been so naughty? Not if she lived for a thousand years would Esther forgive him for spoiling this wonderful Purim day.

The front doorbell rings but Esther pays no attention. Mama, who understands little girls, announces with a smile, "It is Gerard."

"No!" Esther flees from the room. Mama finally catches up with her in the tiny linen closet at the back of the apartment, but Esther is stubborn.

"No, no, no! He has come too late."

Gerard has come as far as the hallway, but he does not dare to advance any farther.

Esther shouts at him fiercely: "Go away! I don't want to see you any more!"

It is then that little Gerard bursts into tears and says in a choking voice: "Esther, I have brought you a rose. I had to break my little bank open to buy it for you."

And that is the end of my story. Undoubtedly, Esther and Gerard will make up, quarrel and make up again. They will grow up and life will separate them but they will not forget the years of their childhood. And even though Esther will not marry Gerard, I think she will always recall with happiness the little boy who, one Purim eve, offered her her first rose.

5. THE PURIM OF SARAGOSA

The King of Saragosa in the country of Spain performed a beautiful custom for those Jews who lived in his realm. Once each year he paid a visit to the Jewish quarter and met with the communal leaders there; he interested himself in their condition, their business, and in everything that went on in the life of the people.

The Jewish citizens of the capital city would receive the king with good grace; the women would bedeck themselves with jewelry, and the men would wear their Sabbath clothes. The synagogue beadle would take the scrolls of the Torah from their holy Arks, and the officers and distinguished men of the community would carry them in front of everyone, to fulfill that which is said, ". . . with the abundance of people is the king enhanced."

But there were to be found those among the officers of the community who saw in this carrying of Torah scrolls in the streets of the city a degrading of Torah, and they brought the matter for judgment before the Jewish community council. After some discussion the conclusion was reached that, on the day of the gathering in honor of the king, the distinguished men of the community should carry only the Torah cases and that the Torah scrolls themselves would remain in the Arks. It was also decided that this decision should be kept secret, lest the king find out and grow angry. But the community leaders were unsuccessful in guarding the secret, and the matter soon was known to all.

Now, there lived in that city an apostate who searched for a way of revenge against his Jewish brethren, those who made fun of him when he left the religion of his forefathers. What did this apostate do? He went to the king and told him what had been decided by the community leaders. The matter aroused the king's anger. "So those Jews are liars!" he cried. "If your words are proven right, I will not rest until I take retribution from those leaders who would fool me and thus dishonor a king who does them good."

When the time for the meeting between the king and the Jewish representatives approached, a messenger of the community council went forth and directed the servants to be ready at dawn and to bring the Torah cases only at the moment when the leaders were about to meet the king.

However, the guardian of Israel does not sleep or slumber. Elijah the prophet, may he be remembered for good, appeared to the servants in the form of a messenger of the community council. He awakened them in the dead of night, led them to the synagogue, and informed them that the community council had decided not to change the custom this one time and that they were to appear as always with the holy scrolls before the king.

The servants did as they were told. The procession began, and the entire community, dressed beautifully, went forth to meet the king. The apostate, too, was among them. The king passed among the people. Suddenly, he stopped before the head of the community and asked him to open the case of the Torah scroll he held in his hand. The faces of the rabbi and the other leaders were ashen. What would happen when the king discovered that they had fooled him?

Imagine their amazement when they saw the Torah scrolls as usual standing in their cases! The eyes of the Jewish leaders brightened—and they all said a blessing over the miracle that had happened to them. And as for the apostate, he became shocked from what he saw, and trembled greatly.

The king beckoned him and said, for the benefit of the astonished leaders, "This man who converted from his forefather's faith has caused the Jews trouble from the time he was baptised. He is the one who brought the evil rumor against you. And now he will be punished. Do to him what he planned to do to you!"

Then the community heads said to the king, "Our Lord, we have no right to judge matters of corporal punishment. He is in your hands." The king commanded that the apostate be put in jail for the rest of his life, and the Jews were full of joy.

As a remembrance of that day, the Jews of Saragosa celebrate this one day of the year and call the day "The Purim of Saragosa."

NOTABLE PURIM QUOTATIONS

1. When Adar comes, rejoicing increases (Talmud, *Taanit* 29a).

2. Rava said: It is the duty of every person on Purim to drink wine until he cannot tell the difference between "cursed be Haman" and "blessed be Mordecai" (Talmud, *Megillah* 7a).

3. Rabbah and Rabbi Zera joined together in a Purim feast. They become intoxicated and Rabbah arose and killed Rabbi Zera. The next day, he prayed on Rabbi Zera's behalf and brought him back to life. Next year, Rabbah said: "Will your honor come and we will have the Purim feast together?" Rabbi Zera replied: "A miracle does not take place on every occasion" (Talmud, *Megillah* 7b).

4. As myrrh (*mor*) is the foremost of spices, so Mordecai was the foremost of the righteous of his generation (*Esther Rabbah* 2:5).

5. Rabbi Joshua ben Levi declared that one of the three things the earthly Court instituted and the Court on High approved is the reading of the *Megillah* (Talmud, *Makkot* 23b).

6. In the time to come, all the other parts of the Prophets and the Writings will lose their worth and only the Torah of Moses and the Book of Esther will retain their value (Jerusalem Talmud, *Megillah* 1:5).

7. Should all other festivals cease to be observed, the days of Purim will never be annulled (*Midrash* on Proverbs 9:2).

8. The collection for Purim must be given to the poor for the Purim festival (Talmud, *Bava Metzia* 78b).

9. Why is Esther likened to the Morning Star? To tell us that as the Morning Star marks the end of the night, so does Esther mark the end of all miracles (Talmud, *Yoma* 29).

10. Haman said to Ahasuerus: There is a certain people scattered abroad and dispersed among the people in all the provinces of your kingdom; their laws are diverse from all people . . . (Esther 3:8).

11. As the days wherein the Jews rested from their enemies, and the month which was turned unto them from sorrow to joy, and from mourning into a good day:

that they should make them days of feasting and joy and of sending portions one to another, and gifts to the poor (Esther 9:22).

12. The Jews had light, and gladness, and joy and honor (Esther 8:16).

GLOSSARY OF PURIM TERMS

Adar: The Hebrew month during which Purim occurs

Adloyada: Literally, "until he does not know . . . the difference between Haman and Mordecai; a frivolous practice of making merry and drinking until one cannot tell the difference between "cursed be Haman" and "blessed be Mordecai." The Purim carnival in Israel is also referred to as *adloyada*.

Ahasuerus: The King of the Purim story

Al HaNissim: A special prayer recited on Purim to thank God for the miracle of the Jews being saved from extermination at the hands of Haman

Amalekites: The ancient people from whom Haman was descended

Benjamin: The tribe from which Mordecai was descended

Esther: King Ahasuerus's Jewish Queen and the heroine of the Purim story

Feast of Lots: Another name for Purim

Five Scrolls: The series of shorter books of the Bible,

161

which are read on certain festivals and fasts and of which the Book of Esther is the most famous

Greggar: A noisemaker used during the reading of the *Megillah*

Hadassah: The Hebrew name of Esther

Haman: King Ahasuerus's prime minister who wanted all of the Jews killed

Hamantachen: A three-cornered pastry that is a favorite food on Purim and is said to resemble Haman's hat

Matanot L'evyonim: Gifts to the poor on Purim

Megillah: A parchment scroll, referring especially to the Book of Esther, which is read publicly on Purim

Mishloach Manot: The sending of gifts to one another on Purim

Mordecai: The cousin of Esther and the hero of the Purim story

Persia: The country of the Purim story. Today it is called Iran.

Pur: A lot or a chance

Purim Spieler: Purim actor

Seudah: The special festive Purim feast, often accompanied by merrymaking

Shushan: The capital city of Persia where the story of Purim took place

Shushan Purim: The name by which the day after Purim is known

Ta'anit Esther: The Fast of Esther

Vashti: King Ahasuerus's first queen

Zeresh: Wife of Haman

FOR FURTHER READING

Bloch, Abraham P. *The Biblical and Historical Background of the Jewish Holy Days*. New York: Ktav Publishers, 1978.

Epstein, Morris and Ezekiel Schloss. *The New World Over Story Book*. New York: Bloch Publishing Company, 1968.

Frankel, Ellen. *The Classic Tales*. New Jersey: Jason Aronson, 1989.

Ganzfried, Solomon. *Code of Jewish Law*. New York: Hebrew Publishing Company, 1961.

Gaster, Theodor H. *Festivals of the Jewish Year*. New York: William Morrow and Company, 1953.

Golomb, Morris. *Know Your Festivals and Enjoy Them*. New York: Shengold, 1973.

Greenberg, Irving. *Living the Jewish Way*. New York: Summit Books, 1988.

Isaacs, Ronald H., and Kerry M. Olitzky. *Sacred Celebra-*

tions: A Jewish Holiday Handbook. New Jersey: Ktav Publishers, 1994.

Isaacs, Ronald H. *The Jewish Family Game Book of the Sabbath and Festivals*. New Jersey: Ktav Publishers, 1989.

Strassfeld, Michael. *The Jewish Festivals*. Philadelphia: Jewish Publication Society, 1985.

Waskow, Arthur. *Seasons of Our Joy: A Handbook of Jewish Festivals*. New York: Summit Books, 1982.

INDEX

Aba, R., son of Kehana, 110
Abaye, 116–118
Abaye the son of Abin, 119
Abba, R., son of Afron, 111–112
Abba, R., son of Kahana, 110–111
Adar I, 10, 20, 49
   fifteenth of, 19–20, 42, 53, 55, 57–58, 73
   fourteenth of, 20, 42, 50, 55, 57–58, 73
   thirteenth of, 12, 41, 49–50, 76
Adar II, 10, 20, 66–67
Adla-yada, 22
Adloyada Carnival, 77
Agag, King, 64

Ahasuerus
   feast of, 7
Ahasuerus, King, 16, 19–20, 26–34, 40–42, 66, 109–110, 115, 116, 121–127, 156
   chamberlains of, 129
   derivation of name of, 124
   identity of, 6, 43–44
Akiva, R., 10–11, 117
Al ḥanissim paragraph, 18
Alkabez, R. Solomon, 7
Alphabet
   in Book of Esther, 77
Amalek, 11, 19, 63–64
Amalekites, 40, 123
Ani Purim, 85
Antiochus, 19

169

About the Author

Rabbi Ronald H. Isaacs has been the spiritual leader of the Temple Sholom in Bridgewater, NJ, since 1975. He received his doctorate in instructional technology from Columbia University's Teachers College. He is the author of more than sixty books. His most recent publications include *Every Person's Guide to Death and Dying in the Jewish Tradition* and *Every Person's Guide to Jewish Philosophy and Philosophers*. Rabbi Isaacs currently serves as chairperson of the publications committee of the Rabbinical Assembly of America and, with his wife, Leora, designs and coordinates the adult learning summer experience called Shabbat Plus at Camp Ramah in the Poconos. He resides in New Jersey with his wife, Leora, and their children, Keren and Zachary.

RECOMMENDED RESOURCES

**Every Person's Guide to the Book of Proverbs and Ecclesiastes:
Biblical Wisdom for the Twenty-First Century**

0-7657-6153-X

**Every Person's Guide to Death and Dying
in the Jewish Tradition**

0-7657-6028-2

Every Person's Guide to Hanukkah   0-7657-6044-4

Every Person's Guide to High Holidays   0-7657-6018-5

Every Person's Guide to Jewish Law   0-7657-6115-7

Every Person's Guide to Passover   0-7657-6043-6

**Every Person's Guide to Jewish Philosophy
and Philosophers**

0-7657-6017-7

Every Person's Guide to Jewish Prayer   0-7657-5964-0

Every Person's Guide to Jewish Sexuality   0-7657-6118-1

Every Person's Guide to Shabbat   0-7657-6019-3

Every Person's Guide to Shavuot   0-7657-6041-X

**Every Person's Guide to Sukkot, Shemini Atzeret,
and Simchat Torah**

0-7657-6045-2

Available at
your local bookstore, online at www.aronson.com,
or by calling toll-free 1-800-782-0015